Project English 3

Student's Book

TOM HUTCHINSON

Oxford University Press

Oxford University Press
Walton Street, Oxford OX2 6DP

Oxford New York Toronto
Delhi Bombay Calcutta Madras Karachi
Petaling Jaya Singapore Hong Kong Tokyo
Nairobi Dar es Salaam Cape Town
Melbourne Auckland

and associated companies in
Berlin Ibadan

Oxford is a trade mark of Oxford University Press

ISBN 0 19 435439 3
© Oxford University Press 1987

First published 1987
Fourth impression 1988

Set in Helvetica Light by Tradespools Ltd, Frome, Somerset
Printed in Hong Kong

The publishers would like to thank the following for their
permission to reproduce photographs:

All-sport; Art Directors Photo Library; A-Z Map Company
Ltd; John Bartholomew and Son Ltd; BBC Hulton Picture
Library; Bettmann Archive; Janet and Colin Bord;
Bridgeman Art Library; Bruce Coleman Ltd; Daily
Telegraph Colour Library; English Tourist Board;
Sir Ranulph Fiennes; Glasgow Art Gallery and Museum;
Sally and Richard Greenhill, Greenpeace; Guinness
Books © Ric Gemel; Michael Holford; The Image Bank;
Mansell Collection; National Galleries of Scotland;
National Portrait Gallery; PGL Young Adventure Ltd;
Rex Features; Royal Collection (reproduced by gracious
permission of Her Majesty the Queen); Scottish Tourist
Board; The Spastics Society; Tony Stone Associates;
Welsh Tourist Board

and the following for their time and assistance:

ABC Cinema, Oxford; Argos, Oxford; 'Biscuit'; CH Brown
& Sons, The Market, Oxford; Café Pelican, London;
Canadian Tourist Board, London; Dell's Fishing Tackle
Ltd, Oxford; Fit Kit, Oxford; Ford Motor Co. Ltd;
Georgina's Café, Oxford; HM Customs & Excise, Dover;
Hoverspeed Ltd, Dover; Jericho Tavern, Oxford; Morrell,
Peel & Gamlin, Solicitors, Oxford; Oxford Archaeological
Society; Oxford Academy of Dramatic Art; PGL Young
Adventure Holidays Ltd; Robinson Cycles, Oxford;
Sarjents Tools, Oxford; The Scouts Shop, Oxford;
Selfridges, Oxford; Sportsplayer/Elmer Cotton,
Summertown, Oxford; St Edward's School, Oxford;
Thames Valley Police; Valentines of Dundee Ltd; FJ Webb,
Butchers, Oxford; White Bros, Outfitters, Oxford.

Studio, location and cover photography by Rob Judges;
Mark Mason; Charlotte Ward-Perkins.

Illustrations by:

David Ace; Martin Chatterton; Laini; Barbara Mullawney-
Wright; Oxford Illustrators; RDH Artists; Chris Riddell; Jim
Robins; Allan Rowe; Techniques Art Studio.

Contents

Topics	Functions	Structures	Student's Project work
Unit 3: NINA (page 31) Theme: Language			
1 People, places, and things	Describing people, places, and things	Relative pronouns (*who, which, that*)	List of people important in your life
2 Carstairs and Carruthers	Coping in a foreign language Explaining Reading instructions	Relative clauses Imperative (*don't always, never*)	Make 'A survival phrasebook'
3 Food	Describing a menu Describing a diet Shopping	Containers (*a jar of, a pound of,* etc.) a little/lot of	Describe your own diet
4 Languages	Describing changes Origins of words	Past tense Present perfect Passive (*. . . is spoken*)	Describe the origins of your own language
Unit 4: CLEO (page 42) Theme: Work and leisure			
1 Jobs	Describing a career Stating qualifications	Past perfect a/an + job	Make your own job adverts and interviews
2 Nina's problem	Expressing regret Expressing feelings	I wish I had/hadn't feel look + adjective	Tell the story of something you regret
3 What's on?	Understanding a TV guide Describing types of programmes Stating likes/dislikes	Prepositions (*on, in, at*) what kind of	Make a guide to your own TV programmes
4 Mary, Queen of Scots	Historical narrative Describing family relationships	Past tenses (Revision) Non-defining relative clauses (with *who*)	Tell a story from your own history
Unit 5: PATRICK (page 54) Theme: The Law			
1 Singapore	Stating rules	It is forbidden/ prohibited/not allowed to . . . Gerunds	Make your own set of laws
2 Matt in trouble	Reporting	Indirect statements	Complete the story
3 Carstairs and Carruthers	Reporting Giving evidence	Indirect questions Indirect commands and requests	Write a short play
4 Trouble-shooter	Reporting Complaining Challenging	Indirect speech (Revision)	Make your own news programme

Topics	Functions	Structures	Student's Project work
Unit 6: ANDY (page 65) Theme: Survival			
1 Paradise Island	Comparing advantages and disadvantages Expressing dangers	Modals (all tenses) get bitten/stung, etc.	Make your own 'Desert Island' programme
2 The argument	Weather forecasts Describing weather	Future tense (*going to*) windy, cloudy, etc.	Make your own weather forecast
3 Trees in danger	Describing a process Classifying	Passive a kind of . . .	Write about pollution in your own environment
4 Carstairs and Carruthers	Suggesting Expressing doubt/regret	shouldn't ought to should(n't) have	Make a short play about being marooned
5 Maps	Describing direction/ location Describing shapes	Compass directions Prepositions/ prepositional phrases shaped like . . .	Describe an island
Unit 7: MATT (page 81) Theme: Danger			
1 Canada	Describing a country Expressing quantity	Superlatives Numbers Percentages	Describe your own country
2 First aid	Giving advice Expressing frequency	should/ought to/ make sure you . . . Imperatives might/could twice a day, etc.	Make a dialogue at the doctor's
3 Carstairs and Carruthers	Describing past habits Expressing need	used to . . . have something done	Write a ghost story
4 Risk	Describing lifestyles Expressing chance/risks Expressing frequency, adverbs of time	Comparatives Gerunds Present simple 50 to 1 etc. (*often, never, always* etc.)	Work out risks in your own lifestyle
Unit 8: CINDY (page 94) Theme: Time			
1 Stonehenge	Describing location Describing shapes Giving dimensions	Relative clauses (with *where*) Prepostions (*in, on, on top of*, etc.) *x* metres high	Describe ruins in your own country
2 Carstairs and Carruthers	Expressing dates Greetings	Ordinals Numbers Question tags Merry Christmas	Write your own calendar of important dates
3 Christmas	Describing traditions Expressing time	Dates Present simple/ continuous tenses Time prepositions (*in, on, at*)	Describe your own traditional festivals
4 Biorhythms	Describing feelings Expressing calculations	Adverbs/Adjectives (*likely to* . . .) Arithmetical terms	Work out your own biorhythm chart Make class survey
The Survival Game			

Introduction

🎧 1　In the Middle Ages pilgrims in England travelled to Canterbury cathedral. It was a long journey and on the way the pilgrims told each other stories. Geoffrey Chaucer wrote down some of these stories in a book called 'The Canterbury Tales'.

In this book you are going to read about a modern group of travellers. Like Chaucer's pilgrims, they will entertain their friends. They will tell us about their lives, their work and their interests.

Before you start, look through the book and find some information about the people in the picture:
—　What are their names?
—　What topics will they talk about?
Then choose one of the people and find out as much as possible about him/her.

1

Hi. My name's Andrew. I'm 19 years old. My sister and I run Canterbury Holidays. We take groups of young people on holidays in Britain and abroad. It's very interesting but it's hard work.

Last year we did all the work ourselves. This year we wanted some extra help. So we put this advertisement in the newspaper.

Canterbury Holidays

**IS YOUR LIFE BORING ?
DO YOU WANT A BREAK ?
DO YOU WANT TO TRAVEL ?**

We're looking for tour guides. Don't expect a lot of money. But we can guarantee you won't be bored.

If you're interested, write to Sue and Andrew Gibson, Canterbury Holidays, 39 London Street, Canterbury.

Please send a recent photograph of yourself.

2

Exercises

1 Right, wrong or don't know?

Tick the correct box.

	R	W	D
a) Andrew and Sue's surname is Gibson.	☐	☐	☐
b) Sue is Andrew's cousin.	☐	☐	☐
c) Sue is older than Andrew.	☐	☐	☐
d) Andrew and Sue are students.	☐	☐	☐
e) Andrew and Sue live in London.	☐	☐	☐
f) Canterbury Holidays needs five tour guides.	☐	☐	☐
g) The tour guides will get £50 a week.	☐	☐	☐
h) If you want to work for Canterbury Holidays, you must telephone Sue.	☐	☐	☐
i) You must send a photograph with your letter.	☐	☐	☐

Language spot 1

reflexive pronouns

Complete the table.
(The missing pronouns are all on pages 2 and 3.)

subject pronoun	reflexive pronoun
I	————
you (singular)	————
he	himself
she	herself
it	itself
we	————
you (plural)	————
they	themselves

3 What information do you think people will put in their letters to Sue and Andrew? What questions do you think they will ask?

4 Andrew received a lot of letters. Here is one of the letters.

a Andrew put the information on cards like this. Make a card for Nina and fill in her details.

b What questions does she ask? Compare what Nina says to your own answers to *Exercise 3*.

Name: ....

Address: ....

Sex: .... Age: ....
Nationality: ....
Reasons for applying: ....
....
....

Interests / qualifications: ....
....

45 Caledonian Road,
Birmingham,
BM20 2JE.
26th June 1986.

Dear Sue and Andrew,

I read your advertisement about jobs as tour guides. I'd like to know more about Canterbury Holidays. But first I'll tell you something about myself. I'm 18 and I'm British. I have just left school and I want to study Geology. I don't want to go straight to college or university. I'd like to do something different first. I can drive and I can speak French and Russian. I can cook and I'm quite good at sports, particularly swimming. I'm interested in Geography and Languages.

Can you tell me more about yourselves and the job? What will we have to do? How much will we earn? When do you want people to start? How many tour guides do you need? I hope to hear from you soon.

Yours sincerely,
Nina Day

5 Use the details in the card below to complete Bruce's letter.

Name: Bruce Dixon

Address: Flat 2, 16 Cornwall Street, Earls Court, LONDON SW4A 9BG

Sex: Male Age: 17
Nationality: Australian
Reasons for applying: wants to travel; needs a job or will have to go back to Australia

Interests / qualifications: car mechanic, good at sport, particularly tennis, driving licence

Flat 2,
16 _ _ _ _ _ _ _ _,
Earls Court,
_ _ _ _.
28th June 1986

_ _ _ _ _ _ _ _,

I read your _ _ _ _ _ in the newspaper. I'd _ _ _ _ _ _ _ _ know more about the job with _ _ _ _ _ _ _ _ _ _. I'm 17 and I'm _ _ _ _ _. I want to _ _ _ _ _, and I _ _ _ _ a job or I _ _ _ _ _ _ _ _ _ _ _ _ go _ _ _ _ _ _ _ _ _ _ _ _. I'm very _ _ _ _ _ in cars. I can _ _ _ _ and I can repair them, too, because I'm a _ _ _ _ _ _ _ _ _. I can't speak any other _ _ _ _ _, I'm afraid - only English, but I'm _ _ _ _ at _ _ _ _ _, _ _ _ _ tennis. Can you _ _ _ _ me _ _ _ _ about the _ _ _ _ ?

Yours _ _ _ _ _,

_ _ _ _ _ _ _ _

6

Language spot 2

expressing a wish

| I'd like | to |
| I want | |

What reasons did people give in their letters? Use the cues below to express their wishes.

Example

I'd like to travel.
or
I want to travel.

travel
do something interesting
see the world
practise foreign languages
do something different
meet new people
have a break
do nothing for a year
earn a lot of money
learn more about other countries
have a long holiday
leave home
visit some friends in Italy
go to warm countries
have an easy time

Which do you think are good reasons?

7

Language spot 3

expressing interests

good at
interested in

Make sentences about Nina, Bruce and yourself, using the table.

			sports.
i'm	not very		practical things.
He's	quite	good at	languages.
She's	very	interested in	car repairs.
			art.

8 🎧 3

Sue and Andrew held interviews for the jobs. Sue is talking to one of the people. Make a card like the one in *Exercise 4*. Listen and complete the card.

Your life ↓

This year your project work will be about you and your life. You will be like one of the travellers in the book. In each section you will find some project tasks called 'Your Life'. When you do these you will be able to talk and write about your life, your work and your interests.
Here's your first task.

Write your own letter to Sue and Andrew.

Well you've met the people in our group. Here we are in front of our van. What do you know about each person?

UNIT 1
SUE

1
Hello, I'm Sue. I started Canterbury Holidays with Andrew because I've always wanted to travel. One day I'd like to travel round the world.
What about you? Would you like to do that? These people did.

1 Ambitions

🎧 **2** The first people to travel round the world went by sea. They were eighteen sailors from Spain. They were the only survivors of Ferdinand Magellan's crew. Magellan, himself, did not return to Europe. He was killed by local tribesmen in the Philippines. Nearly sixty years later, the English captain, Francis Drake, repeated Magellan's voyage in his ship called the *Golden Hind*.

The first solo circumnavigation was made by the American, Captain Joshua Slocum, at the end of the nineteenth century. He sailed 46,000 miles (74,000 kilometres). Yet Captain Slocum could not swim!

The first people to fly non-stop round the world were Captain James Gallagher and his crew. They completed the flight on 2nd March 1949. Their plane was a USAF Boeing B-50 bomber. The flight took 94 hours 1 minute.

Two Canadians, Garry Sowerby and Ken Langley, drove round the world in a Volvo 245 DL car in 1980.

Most circumnavigators have travelled round the Equator. Sir Ranulph Fiennes and his companions did it the hard way. Between 1979 and 1982 they travelled round the world via the North and South Poles.

Since Magellan's time people have travelled round the world on foot and by all forms of transport. Some have ridden on bicycles, horses, motorcycles and trains. Others have travelled on sledges, in cars, lorries, submarines and all sorts of ships, boats and planes. In the sixteenth century, Magellan's men took three years to travel round the world. In 1961 Yuri Gagarin orbited the Earth in 89.34 minutes.

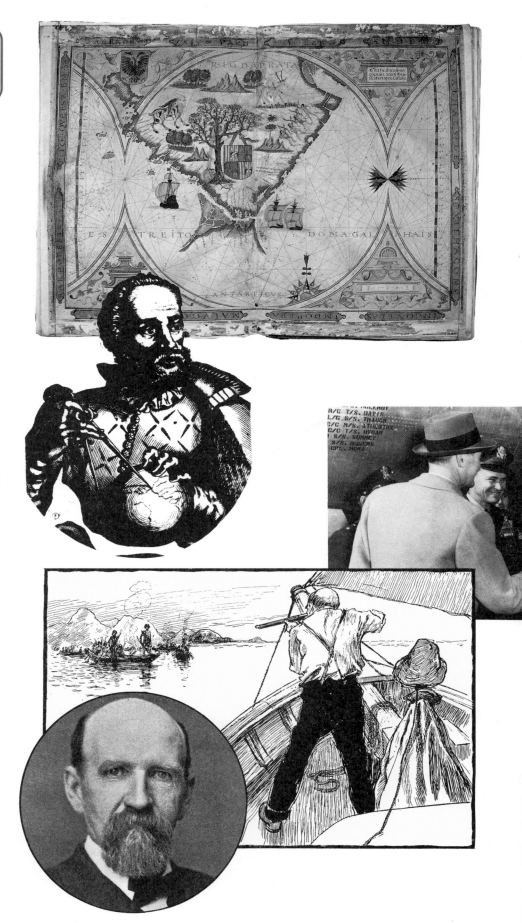

Exercises

1 Right, wrong or don't know?

R W D

a) All the men in Magellan's crew were Spanish. ☐ ☐ ☐

b) Magellan was the first man to travel round the world. ☐ ☐ ☐

c) Magellan's ship was called the *Golden Hind.* ☐ ☐ ☐

d) Captain Slocum sailed round the world with his wife. ☐ ☐ ☐

e) Captain James Gallagher was an American pilot. ☐ ☐ ☐

f) Ranulph Fiennes and his companions travelled North-South instead of East-West. ☐ ☐ ☐

g) Langley and Sowerby began their journey in Canada. ☐ ☐ ☐

h) Nobody has travelled round the world faster than Yuri Gagarin. ☐ ☐ ☐

2

Language spot 1

prepositions

Put these words in the correct tables:

motorcycle foot spaceship
horse plane car ship
sledge

by in a	–––– boat –––– lorry –––– submarine ––––

by on a	bicycle –––– train –––– ––––

on	––––

3

How did they travel? Match the names with the forms of transport. Use: 'in', 'on', or 'by' before the noun.

Example

Yuri Gagarin travelled in a spaceship.

Yuri Gagarin	plane
Ferdinand Magellan	boat
James Gallagher	train
Joshua Slocum	sledge
Ranulph Fiennes	ship
Garry Sowerby	horse
Sir Francis Drake	car
Ken Langley	foot
	lorry
	submarine
	spaceship

4

Language spot 2

verbs of transport

Match these verbs to the correct form of transport in *Exercise 3*:

ride walk sail fly drive

Example

fly: *plane, spaceship*

Say how the people in *Exercise 3* travelled:

Example

Captain Gallagher flew round the world.

5 ⌂3 Listen. You will hear some additional facts about the travellers in *Exercise 3*. Match the facts to the correct travellers.

6

Language spot 3

expressing an ambition: would like to

Complete the table with these words:

would 'd wouldn't like to

What ____ you ____ do?		
I	____ ____ like to ____	travel round the world. have a big car. be a pop star.

7 A mime game: How would you like to travel?

Example

A *I would like to* (mime a form of travel e.g. fly in a plane).
B *Would you like to go by train?*
A *No, I wouldn't like to go by train.*
B *Would you like to fly in a plane?*
A *Yes, I would like to fly in a plane.*

Your life ↓

Ambitions

What would you like to do in your life? What is your ambition?
— Would you like to sail across the Atlantic Ocean in a bath?
— Would you like to fly in the Space Shuttle?
— Would you like to be a famous footballer?

1 Do a class survey to find out what people's ambitions are.

2 The class chooses the best idea. (You can't choose your own idea!)

Exercises

1 Carruthers' diary. Can you complete it?

Saturday 19th June

I was reading a ——— today and I read an article about a ———. He has offered £1 ——— to the ——— ——— to travel round the world. My friend, ——— and I have ——— the race. We will ——— the prize.

Monday 23rd August

We arrived at Victoria ——— at 8———. I watched the ——— while Carstairs went to get the ———. As the train was coming into the station, it ——— ——— a ———. Carstairs was very worried, because he thought it was mine. But it ———. My suitcase was ——— ——— ———. another man's. It was ———. He was very angry. I hope Carstairs' black eye will soon be all right.

2

Language spot 1

possessive pronouns

Complete the sentences:

Example

*This is my bag. It's **mine**.*

That is your bag. It's ____ .
These are her suitcases. They're ____ .
Those are his suitcases. They're ____ .
This is our van. It's ____ .
This is their luggage. It's ____ .

A game

Put some things on the desk: pens, books, pencils, rulers etc.

A picks up one or two things and asks: *Whose is this (are these)?*
B must point to the owner(s) and say:

It's hers. or *They're theirs.* or *It's mine.* etc.

3

Language spot 2

question tags

a Find the question tags for these sentences in the story.

Example

*You like a challenge, **don't you**?*

This isn't our train, _____?
That man has got a suitcase the same as mine, _____?
Hmmm. That's Carruthers' suitcase, _____?
Now you won't be able to go, _____?

b Make a rule for question tags:
– Which verb do you use?
– When is it positive?
– When is it negative?

c [🎧 5] Carruthers is checking some things. Listen and add the correct tag.

4 🎧6 Sue has got a problem. Listen
and find out:

a) What is the group doing?
b) What is Sue's problem?
c) What will she have to do?

What
would you leave,
Nina?

Well, I'd take
the pen, but I wouldn't
take the typewriter. You
don't need both.

hairdryer	blankets	watch	box of matches
sheets	sleeping bag	radio	scissors
towel	washing powder	cassette recorder	penknife
typewriter	soap	comb	tin opener
pen	shampoo	hairbrush	lighter
pillow	toothbrush	needle and thread	
bag	clock	sewing machine	

5

the conditional tense

Complete the tables with these
words:

would   'd   wouldn't

I You He She We They	____ ____ ____	take the typewriter. leave the pens. get rid of the radio.

What	____ ____	you	take? get rid of? do? leave?

6 Sue has to leave some of her
things. She can only take eight of
them. Which things would you take?
Put the items into two columns like
this:

would take   wouldn't take

pen   typewriter

Your life ↓

What would you take on a
journey? Make a list of eight
personal items to take.

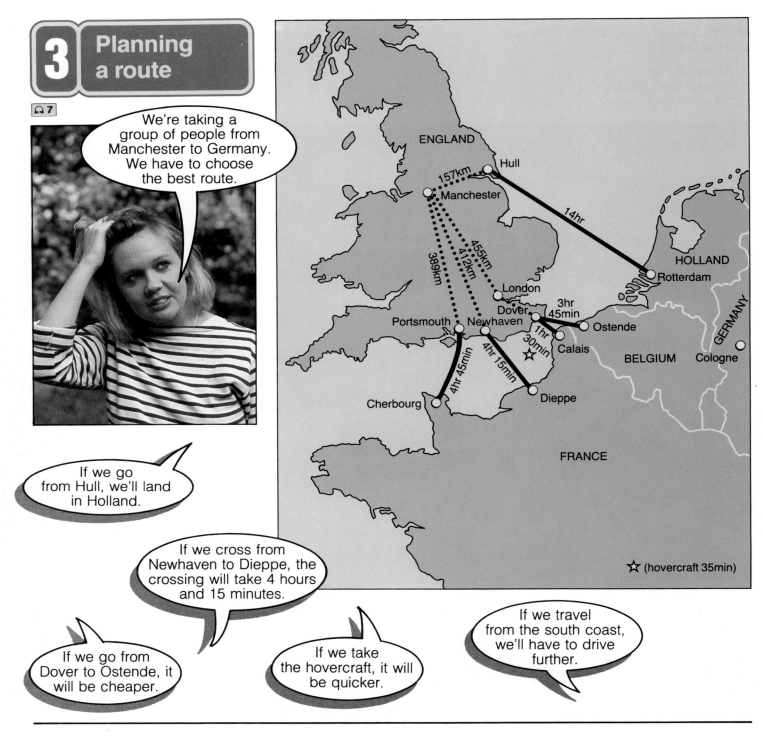

Exercises

1 Match column **A** and column **B** to make true statements about the crossings.

Example

If we go from Hull to Rotterdam, it will cost more.

A	B
go from Hull to Rotterdam	land in France
travel from Dover	be quicker
cross to Calais	cost more
take the hovercraft	take longer
leave from Newhaven	have to go through London
	take less than two hours
	have to drive further
	take 14 hours
	land in Belgium

2

Language spot 1

if clauses 1

This is the **if clause**:	This is the **main clause**:
If we **go** from Dover to Ostende,	it **will take** 3 hours and 45 minutes.
If we **take** the hovercraft,	it **will be** quicker.

– What tense is used in the **if clause**?
– What tense is used in the **main clause**?

3 Ferry tariffs and timetables

a 🎧 8 It can be difficult to read a timetable and work out the right tariffs. Here is an easy guide.

First look at the timetable:
Let's say you want to travel from Dover to Ostende on October 17th. If you take the 7 a.m. ferry, you will pay the D tariff.

Now look at the tariff table:
Look at the D tariff. If there are, for example, two adults and two children, you will pay £11.00 for each adult and £5.50 for each child. (£33.00)
If you have a vehicle, too, you will have to pay the vehicle rate. The longer the vehicle the higher the rate. So, if you have a car 5.00 metres long, you will pay £36.00.
So the total cost for a single journey will be £69.00.
Double this for a return journey. (£138.00)

b Complete the text.

Let's say you want to travel _____ Dover _____ Ostende on October 28th. If you take the 4 a.m. _____, you will pay the _____ tariff. Now look at the tariff table. Look at the E _____. If there are, for example, _____ _____ and _____ child, you will _____ £38.50. If you have a _____, too, you will have to pay the vehicle _____. On this tariff all vehicles cost the same. If you have a car you will pay _____. So the total cost for a _____ journey will be _____. A _____ journey will _____ £113.

DOVER → OOSTENDE

OCT	T W T F S S M T W T F S S M T W T F S S M T W T F S S M T W T
Time from	1 2 3 4 5 6 7 8 9 10 11 12 13 14 15 16 17 18 19 20 21 22 23 24 25 26 27 28 29 30 31
0030 DW	D D D D D D D D D D D D D D D D D D D D D D D D D D D D E E E
★0100 DE	D D D D D D D D D D D D D D D D D D D D D D D D D D D D E E E
0400 DE	D D D D D • D D D D D • D D D D D • D D D D D • E E E
0700 DE	D D D D • D D D D D • D D D D D • D D D D D • D D D D
1115c DW	C C C C C C C C C C C C C C C C C C C C C C C D D D D
★1300 DE	C C C C C • C C C C C • C C C C C • C C C C C • D D D
1515c DW	C C C C C C C C C C C C C C C C C C C C C C C C D D D
1900 DE	• D D D D
1915 DW	D D D • D D D D D • D D D D D • D D D D D • D D D D
★2200 DE	D D D D • D D D D D • D D D D D • D D D D D • D D D D
2330 DW	• D D D D D

c One hour later until 27 October.

NOV	F S S M T W T F S S M T W T F S S M T W T F S S M T W T F S
Time from	1 2 3 4 5 6 7 8 9 10 11 12 13 14 15 16 17 18 19 20 21 22 23 24 25 26 27 28 29 30
★0100 DE	E E • E E E E E • E E E E E • E E E E E • E E E E E
0400 DE	E E • E E E E E • E E E E E • E E E E E • E E E E E
0700 DE	D • D D D D D • D D D D D • D D D D D • D D D D D •
1115 DW	D D • D D D D D • D D D D D • D D D D D • D D D D D

OO

OCT	T W T F S S M T W T
Time to	1 2 3 4 5 6 7
0001 DE	• • • • • • •
0100c DW	D D D D D D
0700 DW	D D D D • D D
★0730d DE	D D D D D • D D
1005 DW	C C C C C C
1350 DW	C C C C C C
★1600c DE	C C C C • C C
1830 DW	D D D D • D D
★1930c DE	D D D D D • D D
2300 DE	D D D D • D D

c One hour later from 27 O
d One hour later from 29 O

NOV	F S S M T W T
Time to	1 2 3 4 5 6 7
0001 DE	E E • E E E E
0200 DW	E E E E E E
0700 DW	E E • E E E E
★0830 DE	D D • • D D D
1005 DW	D D D D D D
1350 DW	D D D D D D
★1700 DE	D • D D D D D
1830 DW	• D D D D D

CAR FERRY TARIFFS Motorist Fares/Vehicle Rates for Single Je

Motorist Fares (driver and accompanying passengers)	DOVER/FOLKESTONE – OOSTENDE				DOVER/FOLKESTONE – CALAIS DOVER – DUNKERQUE				DOVER – B	
	Tariff E £	Tariff D £	Tariff C £	Tariff B £	Tariff E £	Tariff D £	Tariff C £	Tariff B £	Tariff E £	
Adult	11.00	11.00	11.00	11.00	11.00	11.00	11.00	11.00	11.00	
Child (4 but under 14 years)	5.50	5.50	5.50	5.50	5.50	5.50	5.50	5.50	5.50	
Vehicle Rates Cars, Motorised Caravans, Minibuses and Three-wheeled Vehicles*										
Up to 4.00m in length	18.00	26.00	35.00	44.00	18.00	26.00	35.00	44.00	18.00	23.00
Up to 4.50m in length	18.00	32.00	44.00	53.00	18.00	32.00	44.00	53.00	18.00	29.00
Up to 5.50m in length	18.00	36.00	52.00	61.00	18.00	36.00	52.00	61.00	18.00	33.00
Over 5.50m: each additional metre (or part thereof)	9.00	9.00	9.00	9.00	9.00	9.00	9.00	9.00	9.00	5.5
Caravans/Trailers* (not accepted on Dunkerque route)										
Up to 3.00m in length	27.00	27.00	27.00	27.00	12.00	16.00	14.00	12.00	12.00	16.00
Up to 5.50m in length	36.00	36.00	36.00	36.00	12.00	20.00	18.00	16.00	12.00	20.00
Over 5.50m: each additional metre (or part thereof)	18.00	18.00	18.00	18.00	9.00	9.00	9.00	9.00	9.00	9.00
Motorcycles/Scooters	8.00	9.00	10.00	11.00	8.00	9.00	10.00	11.00	8.00	9.00
Bicycles/Tandems	3.00	3.00	3.00	3.00	FREE	FREE	FREE	FREE	FREE	FREE
Cyclists Adult	11.00	11.00	11.00	11.00						
Child (4 but under 14)	5.50	5.50	5.50	5.50						

*50% reduction on selected sailings – see note 3.

FARES NOT AVAILABLE AT

4 These people all want to travel to Ostende on October 22nd. Work out how much it will cost them if they take:

a) the 11.15 a.m. ferry
b) the 10.00 p.m. ferry

Example

If they take the . . . ferry, it will cost . . . .

Your life ↓

Find out about travel connections from your town to neighbouring countries. What forms of transport are there? How long do the journeys take? Which routes are most expensive?

1 Collect timetables and other information about the journeys.

2 Draw a map, showing the routes and journey times.

3 Put some information about prices round your map.

5 🎧 **9** Some people are at the station. Listen and note down:
- *Who?*   - *Single or return?*
- *Where?*   - *How much?*
Note: *a half = a child's fare.*

4 Are you a survivor?

🎧 **10** Some people are very calm. Others are nervous. Some people can stay calm in a crisis. Other people panic. What about you? Are you a survivor? Try this personality quiz.

(Answers are on page 21.)

Exercises

1 Do the personality test in pairs. Write down the answers and scores.

2 🎧 **11** Listen. Nina is answering the questionnaire. Write down her answers. Then say what her personality is like.

Personality quiz

1 If you were on a hijacked plane, would you
a) attack the hijackers?
b) sit still and do nothing?
c) scream?
d) try to escape?

2 If you won a million pounds, would you
a) put it all in a bank?
b) spend it as fast as possible?
c) hide it?
d) tell everyone about it?

3 If you were shipwrecked on a desert island, what would you do first? Would you
a) shout for help?
b) build a hut?
c) look for food?
d) look for fresh water?

4 If a robber attacked you in a dark street, would you
a) give him the money?
b) grab his weapon?
c) scream?
d) run away?

5 If you smelt smoke in the middle of the night, would you
a) go back to sleep?
b) run into the street and shout 'Fire'?
c) look for the fire?
d) telephone the fire brigade?

6 If you saw a car crash, would you
a) faint?
b) telephone the police?
c) help the people in the cars?
d) walk away?

7 If a dog bit your leg, would you
a) forget about it?
b) kill the dog?
c) go straight to hospital?
d) look for the owner of the dog?

3

Language spot 1

if clauses 2

a Notice the tenses:

If you **were** on a hijacked plane, **would you attack** the hijackers?
If a robber **attacked** me in a dark street, I **would scream**.

– What tense is used in the **if clause**?
– What tense is used in the **main clause**?

Write your answers to the quiz in full.

Example

*If I **was** on a hijacked plane, I **would try** to escape.*

b Now look at page 13 (**if clauses 1**).
Why are the tenses different?

Clue: Are the things going to happen?

c What are the short forms?

Which of these are the short forms of the conditional tense?
Positive (**I would**) = I'll, I'ld, I'd, I w'd
Negative (**I would not**) = I'dn't, I won't, I wouldn't, I'ldn't

---

Pronunciation practice

intonation

Look:

My name's Andrew.

Is your life boring?

You like a challenge, don't you?

🎧 **12** Now listen and repeat.

Your life ↓

Make your own personality quiz:
Are you adventurous?

1 Write four questions with possible answers.

2 Write an answer key.

3 Give your quiz to another group. What are their personalities like?

---

4 Here are the answers for the people in the group. One of you is the questioner and the other is one of the people. Role-play their personality tests.

Matt
1d   **2**d   **3**c   **4**b   **5**a   **6**c   **7**b

Andy
1b   **2**a   **3**d   **4**a   **5**c   **6**b   **7**d

Sue
1c   **2**c   **3**a   **4**d   **5**b   **6**a   **7**c

Bruce
1a   **2**b   **3**b   **4**a   **5**c   **6**c   **7**c

5 Say what Bruce and Sue would do.

Example

If Bruce was in a hijacked plane, he would attack the hijackers.

6 Work out the personalities of the group.

That's the end of my tale. Bruce will do the next part. See you.

Mountain View Holiday Centre

MOUNTAIN VIEW HOLIDAY CENTRE

Mountain View Holiday Centre is situated in the beautiful scenery of Wales. Mountain View House was originally the country home of Lord Langdale, but now it has been converted into one of the best holiday centres for young people in Britain.

The House itself has twenty double bedrooms and five single bedrooms. There are bathrooms and toilets on the ground floor and the first floor. There are two kitchens, two dining rooms, a large lounge and a games room.

There is something at Mountain View for everyone. We have facilities for athletics and for playing tennis, football, cricket, volleyball and basketball. The lake provides fishing, swimming, windsurfing, sailing and canoeing. You can go walking or climbing in the mountains. And when the weather is bad, you can play table tennis and billiards indoors, or go shopping in the town. In the evenings there is a disco.

Whatever your interests – from rock climbing to watching TV – Mountain View is the holiday centre for you.

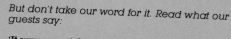

But don't take our word for it. Read what our guests say:

'It was great fun and it wasn't expensive! I had a wonderful time!'
(Jackie, Birmingham)

'We'll be back next year! It was tremendous.'
(Daniel, London)

'Great value!'
(Chris, Edinburgh)

Exercises

1 Right, wrong or don't know?

	R	W	D
a) Mountain View has always been a holiday centre.	☐	☐	☐
b) Mountain View is only for teenagers.	☐	☐	☐
c) Thirty people can sleep in the house.	☐	☐	☐
d) All the bedrooms are on the first floor.	☐	☐	☐
e) There is a television in the lounge.	☐	☐	☐
f) The house stands next to a lake.	☐	☐	☐
g) You can't swim in the lake.	☐	☐	☐
h) When it rains, there is nothing to do at Mountain View.	☐	☐	☐
i) All last year's guests enjoyed their holiday at Mountain View.	☐	☐	☐

2 Which of these can you do at Mountain View?

 skiing

 horse riding

 roller skating

 skating

 throwing the javelin

 boxing

 weightlifting

 swimming

 climbing

 motor racing

dancing

cycling

 running

shooting

 sailing

3

Language spot 1

gerunds 1

I can play tennis.
What kind of word is 'play', a *verb* or a *noun*?

I like playing tennis.
What kind of word is 'playing', a *verb* or a *noun*?

We call words like 'playing', **gerunds**.

Here are some more: skiing, swimming, skating, singing, dancing, climbing, reading, sleeping, eating.

— What do the other members of the group like doing?

Example

Bruce likes climbing.

4
Copy and complete this chart with information about Mountain View Holiday Centre.

Name:
Situation:
Number of bedrooms:
Other rooms:

ACTIVITIES	
Indoors: table tennis,	Outdoors: fishing,

5
What is your favourite pastime? What do you like doing? Conduct a class survey to find the most popular sports and pastimes. Make a graph, showing the most popular sports and pastimes.

Did you hear the joke about the man who wanted to start water-skiing? He gave up because he couldn't find a sloping lake.

Your life ↓

The ideal holiday centre

1 In your group decide what would make the ideal holiday centre for your class. Use the information from *Exercise 5*.

2 Put the information in a chart, as in *Exercise 4*.

3 Make a brochure describing the centre.

2 Warming-up

🎧2 Before starting any activity, you should do some warming-up exercises. If you don't, you'll injure yourself. Here are some exercises. They're good for stretching your muscles.

Stretching

Stand with your feet apart.
Hold your arms straight out level with your shoulders.
Raise your arms above your head. Press your elbows against your ears.
At the same time lift your heels. Stretch up on to your toes.
Slowly lower your arms and your heels.

For the next 2 exercises you will need a chair with a back to hold on to.

Wrist and ankle flexing

Stand behind a chair. Hold the back of the chair with your right hand.
Raise your left arm and your left leg.
Rotate your foot at the ankle and your hand at the wrist. Do this ten times.
Repeat with your right arm and right leg.

Spine, hip and knee bending

Stand with your feet together behind a chair.
Hold the back of the chair with one hand.
Slowly bend forward. Start with your neck, then your back, down to your waist and hips. At the same time lift one knee.
Touch your knee with your forehead.
Lower your knee and slowly stand up straight.
Repeat with the other knee.

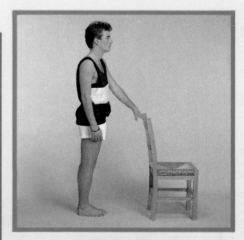

This is very good for your spine.

Exercises

1 Copy this picture. Read the instructions for the exercises and label the picture.

2a 🎧3 Listen. You will hear some instructions. Follow them.

b Now give your partner some instructions. He/she must follow them.

Your life ↓

Make some instructions for an exercise:

1 Give the exercise a name.

2 Write the instructions.

3 Draw some pictures to illustrate it.

4 Say what your exercise is good for.

Answers to personality test (page 15).

Are you a survivor?

0–10: In a crisis you would be cool and calm. You would survive accidents, hijacks and fires. You're a real survivor because you always think of yourself first. But perhaps you would have more friends if you thought more of other people.

11–18: You would stay calm in most crises and you would probably survive. But you would also try to help other people and you would risk your own life. A true survivor would think only of herself or himself.

19–25: You aren't really a survivor. You're too emotional. In a crisis you would panic too easily. If you panicked, you wouldn't be able to think clearly.

26–32: You aren't a survivor at all. In a crisis you would try to be a hero. If someone attacked you, you would defend yourself. You would die bravely, but wouldn't it be better to live to fight another day?

Your score:

1	a)4	b)1	c)3 d)5
2	a)1	b)2	c)4 d)5
3	a)5	b)4	c)2 d)1
4	a)1	b)4	c)3 d)2
5	a)4	b)3	c)1 d)3
6	a)4	b)2	c)3 d)1
7	a)5	b)4	c)2 d)1

21

Exercises

1 Bruce is writing a letter to a friend in Australia. Complete what he says.

> Dear Ken,
>
> We're in _ _ _ _ now. We had an _ _ _ _ today. Before we started, I _ _ _ _ the brakes. The _ _ _ _ shoes needed _ _ _ _, but I couldn't do _ _ _ _ about it then. Later we _ _ _ _ driving along a _ _ _ _ road. Matt was _ _ _ _. The road had a lot of _ _ _ _ and there was a steep _ _ _ _ on one side. Suddenly, as we were going _ _ _ _ a bend, we heard a loud _ _ _ _. We had a _ _ _ _. The brakes wouldn't _ _ _ _ and the van went _ _ _ _ _ _ _ _ _ _ _ _. We _ _ _ _ right on the _ _ _ _ of the cliff. Everyone was _ _ _ _ _ _ _ _. Sue opened the _ _ _ _ and she almost fell out. The van was _ _ _ _ _ _ _ _ the edge of _ _ _ _ cliff. We didn't _ _ _ _ what to do.

2 What should they do? What do you think? Use this table to give advice.

Sue Everybody One of them They	should shouldn't	move to the back of the van. wait for help. go for help. move to the front of the van. sound the horn. shout for help. jump out. drive the van down the cliff. try to reverse the van. climb on to the roof of the van. pray. stay still.

3

Language spot 1

warnings with conditions

If they **move**, the van **might/could** fall.
If they **stay** still, another car **might/could** hit them.

Use the choices in *Exercise 2*. Say what **might/could** happen, **if** . . .

Here are some ideas to help you:

The van might fall.   Sue might fall out.
Another car might hit them.   The van might catch fire.
They might be killed.

4 🎧 **5** Listen. You will hear what happened.

a Note down: Who? What did he/she do?

b Complete Bruce's letter.

New words: axle, rope, tie

5 **What happened to the van?**

Say what happened to the van.

Example   *The headlights were broken.*

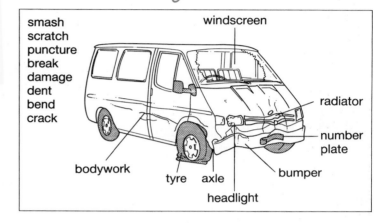

smash
scratch
puncture
break
damage
dent
bend
crack

windscreen
radiator
number plate
bumper
headlight
axle
tyre
bodywork

6

Language spot 2

need + gerund

Can you replace the brake shoes, please?
*The brake shoes need **replacing**.*

Can you check the brakes, please?
*The brakes need **checking**.*

After the accident Bruce took the van to a garage. What did he say?

Use: replace, repaint, repair, straighten

Example
The headlights need . . .

Your life ↓

Write a short play about an accident.

Exercises

1 These are Bruce's and Nina's packing lists.

1 waterproof jacket
2 pairs of jeans
3 T-shirts
3 blouses
2 pairs of shorts
1 pair of trousers
1 pair of boots
2 pairs of shoes
1 swimsuit
6 pairs of knickers
4 pairs of tights
3 bras
1 slip
1 pair of gloves
2 skirts
2 dresses

1 pair of sandals
3 pairs of socks
5 handkerchiefs
2 thick jumpers
1 woollen hat
1 sun hat
1 pair of sunglasses
2 nightdresses
1 toothbrush
1 tube of toothpaste
make-up
hairbrush
comb
towel
bar of soap

1 waterproof jacket
2 pairs of jeans
3 T-shirts
3 long-sleeved shirts
3 short-sleeved shirts
1 belt
1 tie
2 pairs of shorts
1 pair of gloves
2 pairs of trousers
1 pair of boots

1 pair of shoes
1 pair of swimming trunks
6 pairs of underpants
3 vests
1 pair of sandals
5 pairs of socks
6 handkerchiefs
2 thick jumpers
2 thin jumpers
1 woollen hat
1 sun hat

a Which is which?

b What differences can you find between the two lists?

25

2 Look at these pictures of Bruce and Nina. How many of the things in the lists are they wearing?

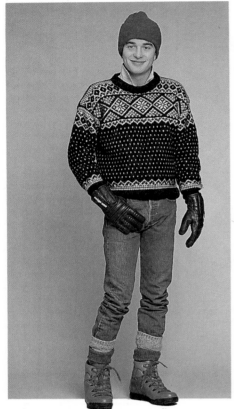

3 Sort the clothes and personal belongings into lists. Find five more items for each list.

Clothes for warm weather:

T-shirts

Underwear:

underpants

Clothes for cold weather:

thick jumpers

Toilet items:

toothbrush

Customer Can I try on that suit in the window, please?
Sales assistant No, sir. You'll have to try it on in the changing room like anyone else.

4

Language spot 1

pair(s) of

Some words are always *plural*, e.g. trousers, jeans.
When we want to say how many, we must use: **pair(s) of**.

a Find all the words in the list that are always plural.

b Complete:
1 *pair of* jeans
3 _____ socks
5 _____ knickers
2 _____ tights
1 _____ boots
1 _____ swimming trunks
4 _____ pyjamas
5 _____ trousers

C A game: In my suitcase

Example

A *In my suitcase I've got one pair of jeans.*
B *In my suitcase I've got one pair of jeans and two T-shirts.*
C *In my suitcase I've got one pair of jeans, two T-shirts and three pairs of socks.*

5

Language spot 2

sizes

a Look at the tables. Write down your measurements in **Continental** and **British** sizes.

	Continental	British
Collar		
Bust/Chest		
Waist		
Hips		
Shoe		

b Look at the clothes in the lists on page 25. What measurements are used for them? Give two examples for each measurement.

c Find someone in the class who takes the same size clothes. Ask:

What size | *shoes* | *do you take?*
        | *jeans* |
        | *shirts* |

or

What is your | *waist* | *measurement?*
            | *chest* |

Shoe sizes (men and women)

British	Continental	British	Continental
3½	36	8½	42/43
4	37	9	43
4½	37/38	9½	44
5	38	10	44/45
5½	39	10½	45
6	39/40	11	46
6½	40	11½	46/47
7	40/41	12	47
7½	41	12½	47/48
8	42	13	48

Men's sizes

Collars		Chest		Waist	
in.	cm.	in.	cm.	in.	cm.
14	36	32	81	28	71
15	38	33	84	30	76
15½	39/40	34	86	32	81
16	41	36	91	34	86
16½	42	38	97	36	91
17	43	40	102	38	97
17½	44	42	107	40	102
18	46	44	112	42	107
		46	117	44	112
		48	122	46	117
		50	127	48	122
				50	127

Women's sizes

Size	Bust/Hip		Size	Waist	
	in.	cm.		in.	cm.
8	30/32	76/81	8	23	58
10	32/34	81/86	10	24	61
12	34/36	86/91	12	26	66
14	36/38	91/97	14	28	71
16	38/40	97/102	16	30	76
18	40/42	102/107	18	32	81
20	42/44	107/112	20	34	86
22	44/46	112/117	22	36	91
24	46/48	117/122	24	38	97
			26	40	102
			28	42	107

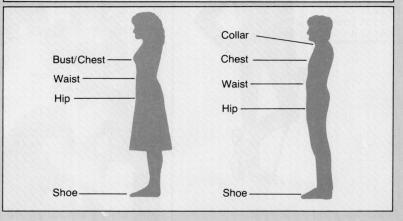

Bust/Chest —   Collar —
Waist —   Chest —
Hip —   Waist —
   Hip —
Shoe —   Shoe —

6 🎧 **7** Listen to the dialogues.

a Complete the chart.

What?	What size?

Example

skirt   *34 inch hips*

b Change the sizes in the chart to Continental sizes.

c Reconstruct the dialogues with the Continental sizes.

Your life ↓

Sizes

1 Find a full-length photograph of yourself.

2 Stick the photograph on a piece of paper.

3 Label the photograph with your sizes in both Continental and British sizes, like this:

```
waist
32 inches
(British)
81 centimetres
(Continental)
```

5 ZERO G

🎧 **8** Have you ever wondered what it is like in a spaceship?

Early astronauts had very little room. This is a Gemini spaceship from 1964.

Modern astronauts have much more room.

There is no gravity in space. This is called zero G. Living in zero G can be difficult.

Eating can be a problem. You can't put the food on a plate and cut it with a knife and fork. When you try to cut the food, it flies away. You have to eat your food from a bag.

Going to the toilet and having a shower are usually easy on Earth, but not in space. Water doesn't fall in space. It floats, because there is no *up* and no *down*. The astronauts need a special shower and toilet.

Some things are easier in zero G. You don't need a bed. You can sleep anywhere. You just fix your sleeping bag to a wall or to the ceiling and go to sleep. You can sleep upside down, if you want to.

You don't need strong muscles in zero G, because everything moves easily. Keeping fit is very important. If the astronauts didn't do a lot of exercises, their muscles would get weaker. Then when they came back to Earth, they wouldn't be able to walk.

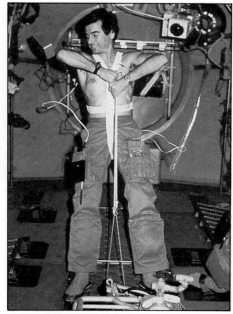

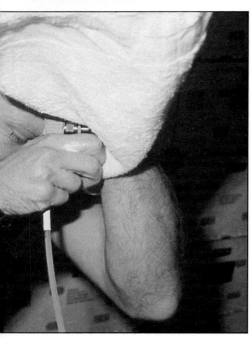

Exercises

1 Match **A** and **B** to make correct sentences.

A

You have to eat from a bag.
You have to take all your air with you.
You need a special shower.
You can't take much with you.
You have to take a lot of exercise.
You have to take everything with you.
Your muscles get weaker.
You can't cut a piece of meat.
You don't need a bed.
There is no up and no down.

B

There isn't much room in a spaceship.
You can sleep anywhere.
Food won't stay on the plate.
Everything moves very easily.
You can't come back for something.
Water doesn't fall.
It will fly away.
There is no oxygen in space.
There is no gravity.
You need to keep fit.

Example

*You can't take much with you,
because there isn't much room in a
spaceship.*

2

Language spot 1

gerunds 2

Eating Taking a shower Cutting food	is	easier more difficult	in space.

Look at the spelling:
eat   eat**ing**
take   tak**ing**
cut   cut**ting**

Spot the differences.
How do the verbs change when you add -**ing**?

a Make the gerunds for these verbs:

skate ski swim box dance keep fit run
get dressed race ride change spell shop
clean

b A mime game
A mimes an activity.
B guesses what the activity is.

3 Which activities do you think are **easier** and which are **more difficult** in zero G?

Example

Taking a shower is more difficult.

take a shower
get dressed
repair the spaceship
take exercise
carry things
clean teeth
walk
go to the toilet
eat
drink
sleep
take photographs
write
run

4 What do you use these things for?

Example

You use a saucepan for cooking.

saucepan   tin opener
sleeping bag   camera
toothbrush   rope
knives, forks   pen
and spoons   hairdryer
spanner
penknife

5 🎧 **9** Listen.

a What activity are they talking about?

Example

1 *Cooking breakfast*

b Listen again. Whose job was it?

Example

Cooking breakfast was Andy's job.

Your life ↓

Some things in orbit can be difficult. But life can be difficult on Earth for disabled people in wheelchairs, too.

1 What things do you think are more difficult for disabled people in your town? Make a list.

Example

getting on a train

2 Recommend some things to make life easier.

Example

Trains should have wider doors.

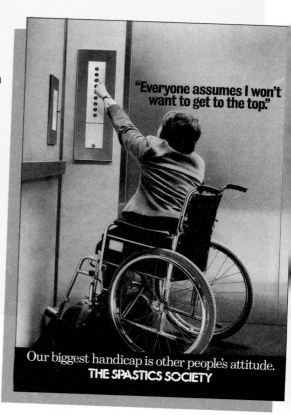

"Everyone assumes I won't want to get to the top."

Our biggest handicap is other people's attitude.
THE SPASTICS SOCIETY

Pronunciation practice

ship or sheep

a 🎧 **10** Listen and repeat.

ship	sheep
this	these
sit	seat
chip	cheap
fit	feet
will	we'll
it	eat

b 🎧 **11** Listen. Which one did you hear?

c Say these:

The king is cleaning his teeth in the kitchen.

The queen is eating fish and chips with her feet.

Jim and Pete will swim in the sea in Greece.

I hope you enjoyed my part of the book. Bye.

NINA

Hello. I'm Nina. I'm the girl who saved the van when it went over the cliff.

I hope you will enjoy the things which I'm going to talk about.

1 People, places and things

🎧2 Have you ever thought about all the people who are important in your life? We don't live with the same group of people all the time. Think of all the different things which you do during the day.

Here are some of the people that you might meet. Give their names.

1 The people that you live with.
2 The people who live in the same street.
3 The boys and girls who sit near you in your class.
4 The doctor who looks after you when you're ill.
5 The people that you don't like (or who don't like you).

They don't have to be real people or people that you really know. These people are important, too:

6 The pop groups that you listen to.
7 The heroes and heroines that you admire.
8 The boyfriend or girlfriend that you dream about.

Perhaps some animals are important in your life, too:

1 The pet which you love.
2 The dog which barks at you.
3 The horse that you would like to own.

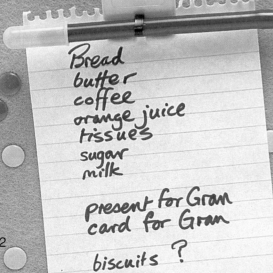

Bread
butter
coffee
orange juice
tissues
sugar
milk

present for Gran
card for Gran

biscuits ?

You don't talk about the same things with all these people. You talk about different things with different groups of people. Would you talk to your parents or your doctor about pop music?

Who would you talk to about these things?

1 some homework which you can't do.
2 some new clothes that you have bought.
3 something which you want to buy.
4 a pain which you have got.
5 the music that you like.
6 a film which you have seen.
7 a dream that you have had.
8 the car that you would like to own.

Exercises

1a Which of the people, animals and things in Nina's life are shown or mentioned in the pictures?

b Answer Nina's question about things that you would talk about.

2

May 1987

Dappled in Light   Rosemary Welch

fri	1	cinema	7.30
sat	2		
sun	3	ring Peter!	
mon	4		
tue	5		
wed	6		
thu	7	slimming class	8.00
fri	8		
sat	9	riding	2.00pm
sun	10		
mon	11		
tue	12		
wed	13		
thu	14		

sat	16	riding	3.30pm
sun	17		
mon	18		
tue	19		
wed	20	* Gran's birthday	
thu	21		
fri	22	To Gran's for the weekend	
sat	23		
sun	24		
mon	25		
tue	26		
wed	27		
thu	28		
fri	29		
sat	30		
sun	31		

Language spot 1

relative pronouns: who, which, that

a Put in the correct word to complete the rule.

who   which   that

We use _____ for things and animals.
We use _____ for people.
We use _____ for people, things and animals.

b Nina is showing some photographs. Use this table to make correct statements.

	clothes things animals tools places people	who that which	helped us. worked at the holiday centre. we took with us. we met on our journey. we saw in Wales. we visited.
These are the			

3 A memory test

Can you remember who it was?

Example

had too much luggage
It was Sue who had too much luggage.

bought the wrong clothes
comes from Australia
is studying to be a doctor
started Canterbury Holidays
drove the van over a cliff
lives in Birmingham
is a mechanic
made the first solo journey round the world

33

4 A puzzle

Read the clues and name the men.

The man who is wearing a hat isn't John.
The man who is standing beside Roy and Nelson isn't wearing glasses.
The man who is holding a camera isn't standing next to the man who is called Roy.
The man who is standing next to the man who has got a moustache is called John.
The man who is wearing a white T-shirt isn't called John.
The man who is holding a camera isn't Keith.
The man who is standing next to Nelson isn't wearing a hat.
Keith is standing between Roy and the man who is standing next to Peter.

5 A game

Find someone in the class who . . .

went to the cinema yesterday.
has got two brothers.
likes the Beatles.
can swim 100 metres.
has been abroad.
can say 'Hello' in French.
is afraid of heights.
knows the first ten letters of the English alphabet.
likes ice cream.
lives in a flat.

Your life ↓

1   Make your own list of the people, places and things that are important in your life. Give examples of each.

People who are important in my life	Places which are important in my life	Things which are important in my life

2   Compare your list with other people's.

6 ⌂3 Listen.

a Who is Nina talking to? Match these people to the dialogues.

The woman who lives next door.
A Spanish boy who is studying in Britain.
Someone that she doesn't like.
The man who works in the newsagent's.
Someone who went to the same school.
A baby that she is looking after.
Someone who wants to work for Canterbury Holidays.

Question Where does Thursday come before Wednesday?
Answer In the dictionary.

b What are they talking about?

Exercises

1 You won't always know the right word for things in English. Then you have to describe the thing which you want. How would you describe these?

a blanket	a saucepan
a knife	a dictionary
a dentist	make-up
a brake	a pilot
a tour guide	a chemist's
an umbrella	a toothbrush
a post office	a battery

Use these expressions:
It's a place which . . .
It's something which . . .
It's someone who . . . .

2 You want to find the places or buy the things in *Exercise 1.* Use your answers to make dialogues like this:

A *What do you call the place which sells stamps?*
B *It's called a post office.*

3 A game

A You are in a shop. You want to buy something but you don't know its name. Describe it.
B You are the shop assistánt. You must guess what the customer wants.

4 A game

Test your friends with some words from your language.

Example

A What is a . . . called in English?
B It's called a . . . .
But remember: *You must know the meaning of any word you ask about.*

5 Read the instructions and find the meanings of these words:

plug　socket　flex　adaptor　fuse
switch　appliance　unplug　switch off

🎧 5

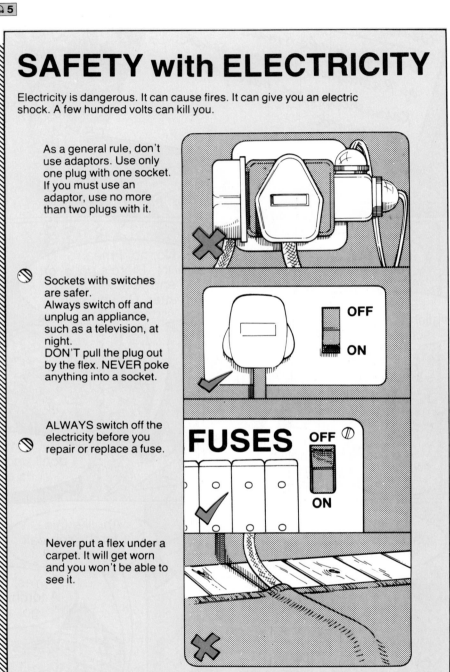

SAFETY with ELECTRICITY

Electricity is dangerous. It can cause fires. It can give you an electric shock. A few hundred volts can kill you.

As a general rule, don't use adaptors. Use only one plug with one socket. If you must use an adaptor, use no more than two plugs with it.

Sockets with switches are safer.
Always switch off and unplug an appliance, such as a television, at night.
DON'T pull the plug out by the flex. NEVER poke anything into a socket.

OFF

ON

ALWAYS switch off the electricity before you repair or replace a fuse.

FUSES　OFF

ON

Never put a flex under a carpet. It will get worn and you won't be able to see it.

Your life ↓

A survival phrasebook

Make a phrasebook for your language for English-speaking tourists. You can have six useful expressions and twenty vocabulary items.

I'll ask this woman.

What did I say wrong?

Ah. It says, 'Be careful with this expression. If you pronounce it wrongly, it means: *You smell like a camel.*'

3 Food

🎧 6

It's my turn to do the cooking this week. Here's the menu for today:

Breakfast
orange juice
corn flakes
toast
yoghurt
coffee, tea or milk

Lunch
tomato soup
cheese sandwiches
salad
tea

Dinner
fried chicken with vegetables and rice

apple pie
coffee or tea

Supper
toast
biscuits
hot chocolate

And here's my shopping list.

1 jar of strawberry jam
1 jar of marmalade
4 loaves of bread (2 brown, 2 white)
1 jar of honey
10 cartons of fruit yoghurt
2 pounds of sugar
1 pound of butter
2 tubs of margarine

2 pounds of rice
5 bottles of milk
1 tin of hot chocolate
4 packets of biscuits
2 pounds of apples
1 pound of coffee
2 pounds of tomatoes
1 cucumber
1 lettuce
3 chickens
1 pound of celery
1 pound of carrots
2 pounds of cheese
1 packet of tea

Exercises

1 Look at Nina's shopping list for the day. Which meal did she buy each thing for?

Example

Nina bought the strawberry jam for breakfast.

2 🎧 **7** Some people are at the village shop.

a Listen and write down what they bought.

b Use your answers to reconstruct the dialogues.

3 How much do you know about food?

Nina is on a diet.

a Make a chart like the one below. Look at the different kinds of food and put them in the right column.

Things which she definitely shouldn't eat:	Things which she can eat a little of:	Things which she can eat a lot of:
sugar	yoghurt	lettuce

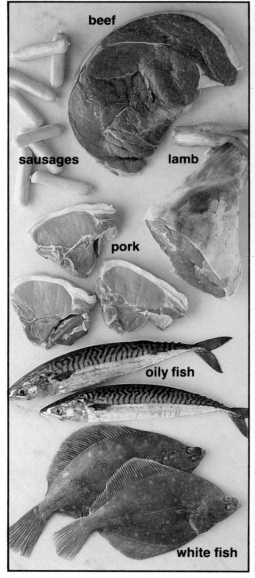

beef
sausages
lamb
pork
oily fish
white fish

potatoes
grapes
garlic
cabbage
melon
peaches
pears
pineapple

cakes
pudding
nuts
bread
margarine
cream
butter
eggs
cheese
sweets
biscuits
noodles
chocolate

b 🎧 **8** Listen and check your answers.

> Note:
> We say   'a little cheese'
>   *but*   'a lot **of** cabbage'

c Look at Nina's shopping list in *Exercise 1*. Add those things to the correct column.

4 Test your memory

Ask and answer like this:

Should Nina eat . . .?
Yes, she should. or *No, she shouldn't.*
or *Yes, she can eat a little.*

Your life ↓

Make a list of all the kinds of food which you eat in one week. Is your diet healthy?

4 Languages

🎧 **9** About 6,000 years ago in southern Russia, lived a tribe of people whose language is known as Indo-European. This language is now extinct, but it was the ancestor of many modern languages which are spoken in every continent of the world today.

We do not know when the Indo-Europeans left their homeland. They travelled both to the north-west into Europe and to the south-east into Iran and India. In modern times, the languages of Europe have been taken across the oceans to America, Australia and Africa. The modern Brazilian speaks a language that is distantly related to the Slavonic languages, like Polish and Russian, to Punjabi, which is spoken in India, and to Farsi, which is spoken in Iran.

The Indo-European family of languages has nine branches: Indo-Iranian, Celtic, Romance, Germanic, Slavonic, Greek, Albanian, Armenian and Baltic. Some of these groups contain many languages. For example, the Romance group contains seven languages including French, Spanish, Portuguese and Italian. These are all descended from Latin, which is now dead. The Germanic group contains two branches: the Scandinavian languages (Norwegian, Icelandic, Danish and Swedish), and the German languages (Dutch, German and English). Some other branches of the Indo-European family, however, contain only one language, for example, Greek, Albanian and Armenian.

The importance of these languages has changed a lot through history. In Roman times, the Celtic languages were spoken from Greece to the North of Scotland. Today, there are only a few speakers in the west of Britain (Welsh and Gaelic), in Ireland (Irish) and in France (Breton). In contrast, Old English was spoken by only a few tribes in northern Germany in Roman times. Today English is the most widely spoken language in the world.

Sanskrit *(an ancient Indian language)*:	pitar	matar
Latin:	pater	mater
German:	Vater	Mutter
English:	father	mother

Exercises:

1 Right, wrong or don't know?

	R	W	D
a) The Indo-European family of languages came from India.	☐	☐	☐
b) The people in southern Russia today still speak Indo-European.	☐	☐	☐
c) Punjabi is spoken in Brazil.	☐	☐	☐
d) No Indo-European languages are spoken in Africa.	☐	☐	☐
e) All the branches of the Indo-European family contain seven languages.	☐	☐	☐
f) Portuguese is a Romance language.	☐	☐	☐
g) The Celtic languages were more widely spoken in Roman times.	☐	☐	☐
h) Portuguese and Spanish are only distantly related.	☐	☐	☐
i) English is spoken by everyone in the world.	☐	☐	☐

2 Complete the chart. Find the names that are missing from it.

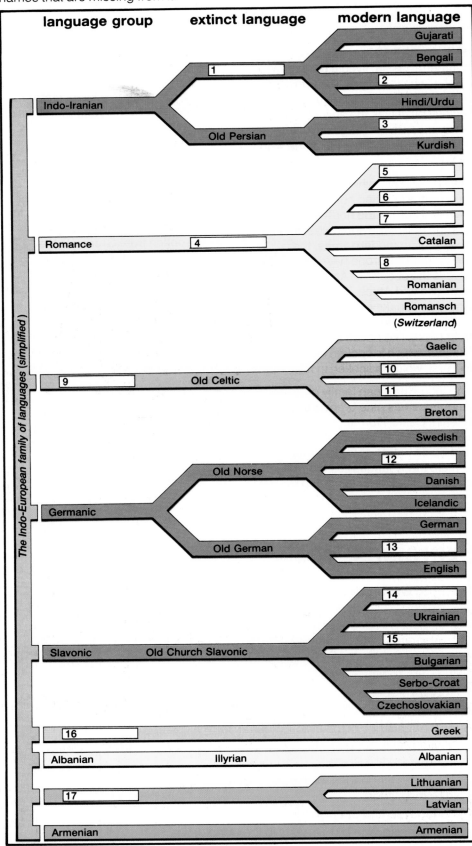

language group	extinct language	modern language
		Gujarati
	1	Bengali
		2
Indo-Iranian		Hindi/Urdu
	Old Persian	3
		Kurdish
		5
		6
		7
Romance	4	Catalan
		8
		Romanian
		Romansch (Switzerland)
		Gaelic
9	Old Celtic	10
		11
		Breton
		Swedish
	Old Norse	12
		Danish
		Icelandic
Germanic		German
	Old German	13
		English
		14
		Ukrainian
		15
Slavonic	Old Church Slavonic	Bulgarian
		Serbo-Croat
		Czechoslovakian
16		Greek
Albanian	Illyrian	Albanian
		Lithuanian
17		Latvian
Armenian		Armenian

The Indo-European family of languages (simplified)

3 Test your knowledge

What are the main languages spoken in these countries?

America	Spain
Canada	Sweden
England	Greece
France	Denmark
Germany	Austria
Italy	Australia
Ireland	Norway
Belgium	the Netherlands
Portugal	Brazil
Poland	Mexico
Scotland	Russia
Switzerland	Argentina

Example

Spanish is spoken in Mexico.

4 🎧 **10** All languages borrow words from other languages. Listen and find out where these English words came from:

pyjamas	and	language
robot	hotel	hotel
coffee	man	summer
bungalow	sky	helicopter
tea	parliament	example
house	bank	get
sugar	temperature	guitar

5 Make a list of words that your language has borrowed from other languages.

6 A memory test

Most languages have a lot of different dialects. Different names are used for the same thing. For example, many common things have different names in British and American English. Look at the two lists below:

British	American
pavement	sidewalk
chemist	drug store
car	automobile
petrol	gasoline (gas)
railway	railroad
trousers	pants
taxi	cab
flat	apartment
policeman	cop
aeroplane	airplane
lift	elevator
shop	store

Some words are spelt differently, too:

colour	color
tyre	tire
programme	progam
tonight	tonite

a Study the two lists for 1 minute.

b Now close your books and ask questions:

Example

What is a car called in America?
How is tyre spelt in Britain?

Your life ↓

Our language

Write about your language.

1 Where does it come from?

2 Which language family does it belong to?

3 What words has it borrowed?

4 Give examples of dialect differences.

Pronunciation practice

'u' and 'oo'

a ⌂ 11 Listen and put the words in the correct column:

supper	book	fuse	noodles

pudding	cucumber	useful
tools	sugar	plug
butter	nuts	Europe
rule	food	toothbrush
honey	look	would

b ⌂ 12 Listen and check your answers.

c Listen again and repeat.

I wonder what languages you speak? Good luck with your English anyway! Bye.

UNIT 4

CLEO

1 Jobs

🎧1 Hello. My name's Cleo Robbins. You haven't met me before. I first met Nina and the others in Scotland. I was a singer with a pop group at a hotel there. Or to be correct, I had been a singer with a pop group at a hotel there. But I had had a big argument with the group's manager and he had fired me. I wasn't too unhappy because I hadn't earned a lot of money with the group. In fact, the argument had been about money. I had wanted more money. Anyway, now I was unemployed and I needed a job. I had just come out of the job centre when I saw Nina.

Exercises

1 Right, wrong or don't know?

	R	W	D
a) Nina met Cleo in England.	☐	☐	☐
b) Cleo had lived in Scotland for a year.	☐	☐	☐
c) Cleo had played the guitar with a pop group.	☐	☐	☐
d) Cleo had lost her job with the pop group.	☐	☐	☐
e) She had had an argument with the hotel manager.	☐	☐	☐
f) The pop group had found another singer.	☐	☐	☐
g) Cleo was looking for a job.	☐	☐	☐

2

Language spot

the past perfect tense

a Look at these sentences. Which ones happened first?

Cleo was unemployed.
Cleo had been a pop singer with a group.

Cleo met Nina outside the job centre.
Cleo had gone to the job centre to look for a new job.

b Complete this statement with one of the following:

after   before   at the same time as

We use the PAST PERFECT to show something happened _____ the PAST.

c Find all the examples of the **past perfect** in Cleo's story.

d How do you make the **past perfect tense**?

3 What had they done before they worked for Canterbury Holidays?

Example

Nina/be at school
Nina had been at school.

Matt/study Medicine for a year
Bruce/have a job as a car mechanic
Sue/work in an office
Andy/be unemployed
Carstairs/travel to the North Pole and back
Carruthers/live with a tribe of Indians

Put in the correct punctuation to make sense of this:

In the test John had had had and Jane had had had had had had had been right.

There's a clue on page 44.

In the test John had had had and Jane had had had had. Had had had been right.

4a 🎧2 Cleo is at the job centre. Copy the table. Then listen and complete it.

Name: ....
....
Address: ....
....
Pay: ....
Last job: ... *pop singer* ....
Reason for leaving: ....
....
....
Qualifications: ....
....
....
Previous experience: ....
....
....
....

b Now say what we know about Cleo.

Example

Before she met Nina, Cleo had been a pop singer.
She had worked . . .

c Use your chart to reconstruct the dialogue at the job centre.

Note: £10 p.a. = £10 per annum
or
£10 a year

min. = minimum

5 Here are some of the jobs advertised at the job centre:

🎧3

JOB CENTRE

Waiter/waitress

Pay: £50 p.w. plus tips
Qualifications required:
O-level Maths preferred, training given

JOB CENTRE

Clerk/typist

Salary: £4000 p.a.
Qualifications required:
5 O-levels, including Maths and English. One year's experience preferred

JOB CENTRE

Secretary

Salary: £5500 p.a.
Qualifications required:
1 A-level preferred: minimum 5 O-levels, inc. Maths, English and French. Min. two years' experience

JOB CENTRE

Carpenter's assistant

Pay: £45 p.w.
Qualifications required:
none: training given; must be good with hands

JOB CENTRE

Petrol pump attendant (part-time)

Pay: £50 p.w.
Qualifications required:
O-level Maths preferred

JOB CENTRE

Receptionist

Pay: £70 p.w.
Qualifications required:
min. 4 O-levels; pleasant manner

JOB CENTRE

Hairdresser's assistant (full-time)

Pay: £50 p.w.
Qualifications required:
O-level Maths and English preferred, training given

a Use the information about Cleo to choose a job for her. Explain your choice.

b The clerk at the job centre is explaining the jobs to Cleo. Look at the conversation below. Now make a conversation between Cleo and the clerk for one of the other jobs.

Man Here's a job as a hairdresser's assistant.
Cleo How much is the pay?
Man £50 a week.
Cleo Hmm, that's not much. Do you need any qualifications?
Man They would prefer someone with O-level Maths and English.
Cleo Is any experience required?
Man No. Training will be given.
Cleo Well, I'll think about that one. Have you got any more jobs?

6 A game: Find someone who . . .

a Write down as many names of jobs as you know. See who can get the longest list.

b Choose one of the jobs, e.g. a nurse, a carpenter. Write the name down but don't show your job to anyone.

c See who can be first in the class to find all of the following:

someone who works in a hospital
someone who drives something
someone who works in entertainment
someone who makes or repairs things
someone who works in an office

Your life ↓

Job centre

1 Make some cards showing jobs in your town.

2 One of you is the clerk. The other is looking for a job. Make the interview.

2 Nina's problem

Nina I'm feeling homesick and depressed. I wish I hadn't taken this stupid job. I wish I'd stayed at home.

Cleo Why?

Nina I got a letter from my boyfriend, Peter, this morning. He says he doesn't love me any more and he's going to get engaged to my best friend.

Cleo The rat!

Nina No, it's not his fault. I can't blame him. He didn't want me to take the job with Canterbury Holidays. He wanted me to stay at home.

Cleo But it's your life. You have to make your own decisions.

Nina Yes, I suppose you're right. I took the job because I wanted to. But after I'd left home, Peter felt very miserable. Then he and Carol went out together a few times and now they're . . . I feel so unhappy.

Cleo Come on. There's no need for tears. You'll get over it. You'll feel better tomorrow.

Nina I'm sorry. I shouldn't cry. You must feel embarrassed.

Cleo It doesn't matter.

Exercises

1 Here's Nina's letter. Can you complete it?

> ☐ Nina,
>
> I don't want to ☐ this ☐, but I'm afraid I must. You know that I didn't ☐ you to take the ☐ with Canterbury ☐. I wanted you ☐ stay ☐. Of course, it's your ☐ and you must ☐ your own ☐. You took ☐ job because you ☐ to. But you know that after you ☐ left home, I felt very ☐. One day I met your ☐, Carol. We went out ☐ a few times and now... well now... I'm sorry, Nina. I don't ☐ you any more. I love ☐, and we're going to ☐ ☐ next month.
>
> You might feel very ☐ when you get this letter, but you'll get ☐ it. I hope that ☐ can still be friends.
>
> Good luck with your job.
>
> Yours, ☐
>
> P.S. Carol sends her love.

3 What do you think Nina should do? Write her reply to Peter.

4

Language spot 2

describing feelings and looks

a Find words in the story to fill the blanks.

I	feel 'm feeling don't feel 'm not feeling	well _____ _____ _____
He She	looks doesn't look	angry _____
You	look don't look	happy _____ worried

b Ask people in the class: *How do you feel today?*

2

Language spot 1

expressing regret: I wish I had/hadn't

a What tense is this?

I wish I **hadn't taken** this job.
I wish I **had stayed** at home.

b 🎧 **5** Listen. What will these people say?

Example

I wish I hadn't broken the window.

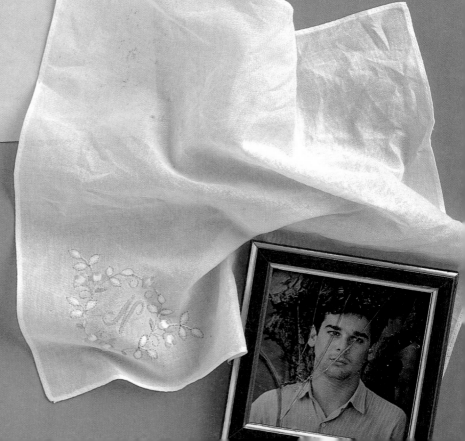

5 Carstairs' and Carruthers' journey

a Look at these pictures. How did Carstairs feel?

Example

He felt happy when Carruthers missed the train in Turkey.

b What did Carstairs or Carruthers say?

Example

I wish I hadn't missed the train in Turkey.

6 A game: Face mimes

A mimes an expression.
B asks, *'Do you feel sad?'*
A answers, *'Yes'* or *'No'*.

7 🎧 **6** Listen. You will hear a story about a man called Llewelyn and his dog, Gelert. After each part you will hear a bell. When you hear it, say:
a) What happened?
b) How did Llewelyn feel?
c) What did Llewelyn wish?

Some words to help you: forest, prince, wolf, deer, throat

Your life ↓

Have you ever wished you hadn't done something? Tell the story.

1 What did you do?

2 What do you wish you had done?

3 How did you feel?

---

3 **What's on?** 🎧 **7**

When I was singing with the group, I couldn't watch television very often. I worked in the evening. But tonight I can spend the evening in front of the box.

🎧 **8**

Now let's have a look in the programme guide. What's on at 8 o'clock?

TONIGHT'S TV

BBC1

7.50 **Tom and Jerry** (a cartoon)
8.00 **Top of the Pops:** the hits from the charts with DJ Clive Sawyer
8.30 **Only Fools and Horses** (a comedy)
9.00 **News; weather**
9.30 **Film:** *'The Reptiles'* (a science fiction thriller) starring Elizabeth Mount and Doug Stanton
11.05 **Sport:** football; show jumping
11.50 **Late film:** *'They Call Me Trinity'* (a western) starring Bud Spencer and Terence Hill
1.30 **Weather forecast**

ITV

7.30 **Coronation Street** (a soap opera)
8.00 **Full House** (a quiz programme)
8.45 *'The Black Flowers'*, episode 5 (a mystery serial)
10.00 **News**
10.30 **Film:** *'My Fair Lady'* (a musical) starring Rex Harrison and Audrey Hepburn
12.30 **Closedown**

BBC2

7.45 **Acid Rain:** a documentary about the pollution which is destroying Europe's forests
8.30 **Opera:** Wagner's *'Ring'* cycle
11.00 **Newsnight:** current affairs
12.00 **Late film:** *'Pork Chop Hill'* (a war film) starring Gregory Peck
1.30 **Closedown**

Channel 4

8.00 **Upstairs, Downstairs** (a historical series)
9.00 **Hill Street Blues** (an American police series)
10.00 *'Mr and Mrs Edgehill'* (a play) by Noel Coward
11.30 **Late night music:** jazz

Exercises

1 Which programme is it from?

In episode 4 MacDuff mysteriously disappeared after Jones had been arrested by the police.

Over to David Coleman at Wembley for tonight's game between England and Brazil.

Now, for fifty pounds, what is the capital of Japan?

Look at this oak tree, for example. The leaves should be green, but they are turning yellow.

The Prime Minister of Canada arrived in London today.

OK, Blue eyes, you're under arrest for the murder of Mrs Kelly.

And this week's number one is *Baby, baby* by Fat Cat.

Tomorrow it will be cloudy in the South with rain spreading from the West later.

2

Language spot 1

prepositions

on, in or **at**

a) What's ____ the box tonight?
b) We have lunch ____ 1 o'clock.
c) What's ____ ITV ____ 9 o'clock?
d) Look ____ the programme guide.
e) Programmes ____ BBC2 finish ____ half past one ____ the morning.
f) There's a film ____ now.
g) Who's ____ the play ____ Channel 4 ____ ten o'clock?

3 Test your memory

Read the programme guide for 1 minute. Then close your book. Now ask and answer.

Example

A *What's on BBC2 at 11 o'clock?*
B *'Newsnight'.*
or
A *What channel is 'Newsnight' on?*
B *BBC2.*

4 Plan your evening. Which programmes would you watch?

Example

At _____ I would watch _____ .

5 [9] Listen. What kind of programme is it?

Example

'Edge of Darkness'
'Edge of Darkness' is a serial.

'Blockbusters'
'Wildlife on One'
'City Under the Sea'
'Porridge'
'Pebble Mill'
'The Motorcycle Man'
'The Horse Soldiers'
'Eastenders'

6 Find out what kinds of programmes people in your class like. Make a list of the most popular types of programme.

Your life ↓

1 Find out what's on TV in your country tonight.

2 Make a guide to the programmes.

3 Find out what people in your class are going to watch.

4 Mary, Queen of Scots

🎧 10

I come from Scotland, so I'm going to tell you a story about the last Queen of Scotland.

Her name was Mary Stuart, but she is usually called Mary, Queen of Scots. It's a very sad story.

🎧 11 In 1542 James V, the King of Scotland died. His daughter, Mary, who was only one week old, became Queen. While she was still only a child, Mary Stuart married Francis, the son of the French King. In 1559 Francis became King of France. So at the age of 17, Mary, who was a beautiful woman with lovely red hair, was Queen of two countries.

But after only one year as King, Francis died. Her mother-in-law, Mary of Guise, did not want Mary in France and so she returned to Scotland.

She married again. This time she married her cousin, Lord Darnley. Mary and Darnley did not like each other. Darnley became very jealous of an Italian, called Riccio, who was Mary's secretary. One night, Darnley and a group of his friends murdered Riccio in front of Mary.

Two years later, Darnley, too, died. Mary had gone to a dance, but her husband was ill and stayed at home. In the middle of the night the house where Darnley was asleep exploded and caught fire. But Darnley's body was not found in the house. It was found in the garden. He had been strangled.

Who was the murderer? People suspected the Earl of Bothwell, but it could not be proved. Then Mary

shocked the people of Scotland. She married Bothwell. This was too much for the Scots. There was a rebellion and the Scottish people made Mary's

son, James, King. Bothwell, who escaped to Norway, went mad and died in prison. Mary escaped to England.

The English Queen, Elizabeth, who was Mary's cousin, welcomed Mary, but the English lords did not trust the beautiful Scottish Queen. She was put in prison and then, finally in 1587, she

was beheaded for treason. When the executioner lifted up her head, he picked up only the hair. It was a wig. Mary's own beautiful red hair had turned thin and grey.

In the end, Mary had lost everything. She had lost the crowns of France and Scotland, three husbands, her son, her life – even her famous beauty.

Exercises

1 Here are the people mentioned in Mary's story.

a Number them in the order they appear in the story.

Elizabeth   Bothwell
Riccio   the French King
James V   Darnley
Mary of Guise   Francis
James

b How was each of the people in **a** related to Mary?

Example

Elizabeth was Mary's cousin.

c Match the names to these sentence endings.

_____ was murdered by Mary's
husband.
_____ died after only one year as
King.
_____ sent Mary back to Scotland.
_____ died when Mary was only one
week old.
_____ was strangled.
_____ died in 1559.
_____ outlived Mary.
_____ was made King by the Scots.
_____ went mad and died in prison.

2

Language spot

non-defining relative clauses

Put your answers to *Exercises 1 b*
and *c* together to make one
sentence.

Example

James V was Mary's father. (*b*)
James V died when Mary was only
one week old. (*c*)

James V, who was Mary's father,
died when Mary was only one
week old.

3 Put these events from Mary's life in the correct order.

Her mother-in-law sent her back to
   Scotland.   (1)
She was sent to France.   (2)
She married Francis.   (3)
Riccio was murdered by
   Darnley.   (4)
She was beheaded.   (5)
Darnley's body was found in the
   garden.   (6)
She escaped to England.   (7)
Francis became King of France.   (8)
Darnley's house exploded.   (9)
She was put in prison by
   Elizabeth.   (10)
She fell in love with Riccio.   (11)
Her father died.   (12)
Her cousin, Elizabeth, welcomed
   her.   (13)
She married Bothwell.   (14)
Francis died.   (15)
She became Queen of
   Scotland.   (16)
Her son was made King.   (17)
She married Darnley.   (18)

4 How do you think Mary felt at each event?

a Use these words to help you:

homesick angry depressed lonely
frightened worried embarrassed
helpless sad happy jealous

b Put your ideas from **a** and the events from *Exercise 3* together to make one sentence.

Example

Mary felt very homesick when she was sent to France.

Customer This restaurant must have a very clean kitchen.
Waitress Thank you, sir. How do you know?
Customer Everything tastes like soap.

5

Language spot

family relationships

Copy and complete the chart. You will find some words to help you in *Exercise 6*.

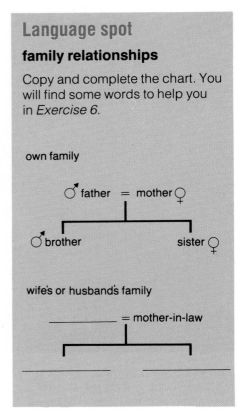

own family

♂ father = mother ♀

♂ brother   sister ♀

wife's or husband's family

_____ = mother-in-law

_____   _____

6 Right, wrong or don't know?

Read Mary's story again and tick the correct box.

	R	W	D
a) Mary had three mothers-in-law.	☐	☐	☐
b) Darnley and Elizabeth were Mary's cousins.	☐	☐	☐
c) Elizabeth's father was Mary's uncle.	☐	☐	☐
d) Mary's father-in-law died in 1559.	☐	☐	☐
e) Mary was Bothwell's third wife.	☐	☐	☐
f) Darnley's mother was Mary's aunt.	☐	☐	☐
g) Bothwell's brother was Mary's brother-in-law.	☐	☐	☐
h) Mary had two sisters-in-law.	☐	☐	☐

7 Families

Find out who in your class has the most:
uncles, aunts, cousins, brothers-in-law, sisters-in-law.

Your life ↓

Tell the story of a famous person from the history of your country.

Pronunciation practice

'h'

a 🎧 12 Listen and repeat:
Hannah the hairdresser has had an unhappy hour at an old hospital in East Hull.

stress

b Look at these words. Mark the stressed syllable:

Example

first	second	third
hospital	un**happ**y	enter**tain**

assistant	secretary
depressed	murderer
boyfriend	rebellion
miserable	executioner
engaged	experience
television	unemployed
football	photograph
coronation	manager
embarrassed	

c 🎧 13 Listen and check your answers.

d Find more words for each group.

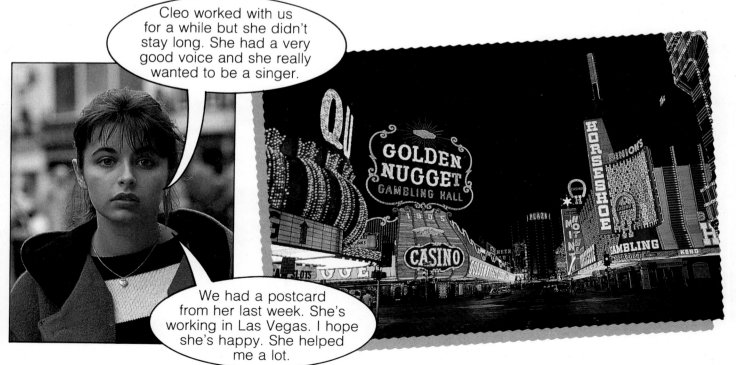

Cleo worked with us for a while but she didn't stay long. She had a very good voice and she really wanted to be a singer.

We had a postcard from her last week. She's working in Las Vegas. I hope she's happy. She helped me a lot.

Hello. My name's Patrick Chan. I'm a friend of Andy's father. I'm from Singapore. I want to be a lawyer and I'm studying Law at the University of Kent, which is in Canterbury.

As you will see, Singapore is a good place for lawyers.

1 Singapore

🎧 2

The Garden City of Asia

Singapore welcomes visitors and tourists. Please respect the laws of this country. Here are some points to remember:

SMOKING: Cigarette smoking is a danger to health. It is prohibited in lifts, cinemas, theatres, all government offices and on buses. Fines of up to $500.

LITTER: Singapore is the *Garden City of Asia* – clean and green. Dropping litter in public places is forbidden. You can be fined up to $500 for dropping litter – even if it is only a sweet wrapper or a cigarette end.

LONG HAIR: Male visitors should not have hair longer than the top of their shirt collar. Long-haired men will be served last of all in government offices.

DRUGS: You can be fined or put in prison for possessing illegal drugs. The penalty for possessing and trafficking more than 15 grams of heroin or morphine is death.

GAMBLING: Only official horserace betting and lotteries are permitted. No other forms of gambling are allowed – even in private houses.

JAYWALKING: You must always use the pedestrian crossings. You can be fined $50 for crossing the street less than 50 metres from a crossing, or for crossing on the red man. These laws also apply to children who are old enough to be in the street on their own.

2

Exercises

1 Right, wrong or don't know?

	R	W	D
a) Tourists do not have to follow these laws.	☐	☐	☐
b) It is illegal to smoke in Singapore.	☐	☐	☐
c) You can be fined $500 for smoking on a bus.	☐	☐	☐
d) Dropping litter carries the death penalty.	☐	☐	☐
e) It is illegal to have long hair in Singapore.	☐	☐	☐
f) Women with long hair are served last in government offices.	☐	☐	☐
g) You can be executed for buying and selling heroin.	☐	☐	☐
h) You are only allowed to gamble in your own home.	☐	☐	☐
i) Children are not allowed to cross the road on their own.	☐	☐	☐
j) You should cross the road only when the pedestrian light is green.	☐	☐	☐

Language spot 1

rules

1 Find words in the text to complete these tables:

Smoking in cinemas is	f_____. p_____. i_____.

You are not _____ It is i _____	to	smoke in cinemas.
You _____ not		

2 Make as many true sentences about Singapore's laws as you can. Use the tables.

> . . . *is illegal.*
> *You are not allowed to . . .*
> *You must not . . .*

3 Carstairs and Carruthers in Singapore

a Look at these pictures. What are they doing? Are they breaking the law? Say why.

b Now say what could happen to them in Singapore. Use this table to make as many sentences as you can.

			taking photographs.
He could be He could not be	fined up to $ . . . executed put in prison	for	crossing on a red light. jay walking. buying drugs. smoking in a cinema. gambling. dropping litter.

4

Language spot 2

gerunds 3

a These sentences all mean the same. One is *informal*, the others are *formal*. Which do you think is the *informal* one?

You are not allowed to smoke in cinemas.
Smoking in cinemas is forbidden.
It is illegal to smoke in cinemas.
You mustn't smoke in cinemas.
Smoking in cinemas is prohibited.

b 🎧 3 Listen and give the *informal* version.

Example

Smoking in cinemas is forbidden.
You mustn't smoke in cinemas.

Crossing on the red man is prohibited.
You mustn't cross on the red man.

5

What do you think of Singapore's laws? What are the laws in your country like for these things?

> **Girl** Would you punish someone for something that she didn't do?
> **Teacher** Of course not.
> **Girl** Good, because I haven't done my homework.

6

Look at these signs. What do they mean? Use the tables in *Exercise 2* to explain.

Example

This sign means walking on the grass is forbidden.

7

Make some signs to show that something is forbidden. Can the rest of the class guess what they mean?

Your life ↓

Make a set of laws to keep your town clean and green.

2 Matt in trouble

Speech bubbles (part of image):
- "I told him I could take it for him, because we were going back to England today and he said that would be very helpful."
- "Get out of the van, please and put your luggage over here."
- "Here we are at customs."
- "This looks like heroin! Wait while I call the police. If it is heroin they'll arrest you for drug smuggling!"
- "Excuse me, sir. Can I see that parcel?"
- "Yes, sure."

2

Exercises

1 This is Matt's statement to the police inspector. Can you complete it?

We have just come back from a ＿＿＿＿ to Europe. While we ＿＿＿＿ in Paris, I lost my ＿＿＿＿. A man ＿＿＿＿ it. He said his name was ＿＿＿＿ ＿＿＿＿ and that he ＿＿＿＿ for the North ＿＿＿＿ Bank. He ＿＿＿＿ he had a parcel for some friends in ＿＿＿＿, but it would be too ＿＿＿＿ to post. I said we were ＿＿＿＿ to England and I said I ＿＿＿＿ take the ＿＿＿＿ for him. When we ＿＿＿＿ at ＿＿＿＿, the ＿＿＿＿ officer wanted to ＿＿＿＿ the parcel. He opened it and found ＿＿＿＿ inside. He told us to ＿＿＿＿ while he ＿＿＿＿ the police. Later, the police ＿＿＿＿ us for drug ＿＿＿＿.

Language spot 1

indirect speech

a Compare these two passages. What differences can you see in *tenses* and *pronouns*?

Direct speech
'My name's Jim Carlson. I work for the North Australia Bank. I've lived in Paris for three years now. I lived in England before that. In fact this parcel is for some friends there. But it will be heavy to post.'
'I can take it for you. We're going to England.'
'That would be very helpful.'
'It won't be any trouble. After all, you found my wallet.'

Indirect speech
He said his name was Jim Carlson and that he worked for the North Australia Bank. He said he had lived in Paris for three years.
He said he had lived in England once and that he had a parcel for some friends there, but it would be too heavy to post.
I told him I could take it for him, because we were going to England. He said that would be very helpful, and I said it would be no trouble, because he had found my wallet.

b Find an expression which means the same as *'He said . . .'*

c In indirect speech, the tenses change. Use the passages to complete this chart:

Direct speech	Indirect speech
present simple	past simple
present continuous	＿＿＿＿＿＿
present perfect	＿＿＿＿＿＿
future	＿＿＿＿＿＿
past	＿＿＿＿＿＿
conditional	＿＿＿＿＿＿

3 🎧**5** Patrick Chan has visited Matt in prison. Matt is telling Andy about Patrick. Listen and give Matt's report.

Example

My name is Patrick Chan.
He said his name was Patrick Chan.

I will be your lawyer.
He said he would be our lawyer.

4 Matt is talking to Patrick. Give Matt's answers to make the conversation.

Example

Where did you meet this man?
I met him in a café in Paris.
How did you meet him?
He found my wallet.

What was his name?
He said _____.
Why was he in Paris?
He said _____.
How long has he been in Paris?
He said _____.
What did he say about the parcel?
He said it _____.
What did you tell him?
I told him we _____.
What did he say?
He said _____.
What did you say?
I said _____.
He probably stole your wallet, so that you would take the parcel for him. It's an old trick.
Oh. I've been very stupid, haven't I?

5 The police inspector is talking to Patrick.

'The French police have arrested a drug smuggler. He said that his name was Jim Carlson. He told the police that he had given a parcel to a young Canadian who was travelling to England. He said that there was heroin in the parcel. He said that he had stolen the Canadian's wallet and then he had pretended to find it. He said that the Canadian was travelling in a van.'

What did Jim Carlson say to the French police? Start like this:
'My name is . . .'

6 🎧**6** The police have investigated the case. The police inspector is telling Patrick what is going to happen. Before you listen to it, what do you think will happen to them? Now listen and find out.

a) What have the police done?
b) What does the police inspector say about Matt?
c) Will Matt be put on trial?
d) What is going to happen to Matt?
e) What is going to happen to the others?

New word: witness

7 Patrick is telling the group what the police inspector said. Give his report.

What did he say, Patrick?
He said that they had . . .

Your life ↓

What will happen at the trial?
Role-play the trial.

Exercises

1 Read the story and find this information:

– What was the *charge*?
– Who was the *witness for the prosecution*?
– What was the *evidence*?
– What was the *verdict*?
– What was the *sentence*?

2 Here is the conversation at the customs. But it's all in the wrong order. Put it in the correct order.

It isn't mine. **(1)**
This is a new camera. Where did you buy it? **(2)**
I've never seen it before. **(3)**
Come with me, please. **(4)**
No, I haven't. **(5)**
It's Carruthers' camera. **(6)**
Whose camera is it? **(7)**
Have you got anything to declare? **(8)**
Open your suitcase, please. **(9)**
Yes, I've got a bottle of wine. **(10)**
Is this your camera, Mr Carruthers? **(11)**
Have you got any alcohol or cigarettes? **(12)**

3

4 Here are the questions which the passport official asked Carstairs.

– Where have you come from?
– What nationality are you?
– Have you got any relatives in Australia?
– Where are you going to stay?
– How long are you going to stay?
– Have you been to Australia before?
– Are you travelling alone?
– Why have you come to Australia?
– Are you here on business or for a holiday?

a Make the passport officer's report.

Example

*I asked him where he had come from.
I asked him what nationality he was.*

b What questions do you think the customs official in England asked Matt?

5

6 🎧 **8** Listen. The English customs officer is talking to Matt and the others after their trip to France. Report what he said.

Example

Get out of the van.
He told them to get out of the van.

Your life ↓

Make the dialogue to fit this scene and the courtroom scene which would follow it.

RABIES PREVENTION

NO PETS

If you bring in an animal illegally you will be liable to an unlimited fine or up to a year's imprisonment.
The animal itself may be destroyed.
☐ If you have an animal with you, even if it has been vaccinated a̶ ̶ ̶ ̶ ̶ies, contact the shipping o̶ ̶ ̶ ̶ ̶
Purser on board ship.

4 Troubleshooter

🎧 9

My favourite radio programme is called 'Troubleshooter'. The reporter on the programme is Roger Dunn. He investigates cases where people have been cheated.

🎧 10

This letter arrived in our office last week. It's from Carol Martin in Liverpool.

18 Prince Road,
Liverpool 9.
25 May 1987

Dear Mr Dunn,

I'm writing to ask for your help. You are the only person who can help me.

Last July, I saw an advertisement in a magazine for the Top Girls model agency. I've always wanted to be a model, so I went to their office in Newgate Street in London. It was a very smart office and I met a man called Mr O'Brien. I told him that I had seen his advertisement and that I wanted to become a model. He asked me whether I had had any experience as a model before. I said that I hadn't. He said that I was a very attractive girl and that he would help me in my ambition. He said that he had helped lots of girls and that some of his models were earning £1,000 a week. He told me to fill in a form and then he asked me to pay a registration fee of £100. I asked him what I would get for my £100. He said that he would take some photographs of me and that he would send these photographs to important people in the fashion world. Then he asked me if I wanted to have some lessons in modelling. I said I would and he said that it would cost another £50. Foolishly I paid the money. He took some photographs, but since then I have heard nothing. I have telephoned several times, but the secretary always says that Mr O'Brien is out or busy. Last week I went to the office again. I waited all day to see Mr O'Brien. When I saw him, he said I should be patient. I said that I wanted my money back. He got very angry. He said that he would write to all the important people in the fashion world and tell them to blacklist me.

Now I don't know what to do. Please help me.

Yours sincerely,

Carol Martin

Carol Martin.

Exercises

1 Roger Dunn telephoned Carol Martin to check the facts. Use Carol's letter to complete their conversation.

Roger Hello. My name is Roger Dunn from 'Troubleshooter'. We received your letter. Can I just check some facts, please?

Carol Yes, of course.

Roger What is your full name and address?

Carol _____.

Roger How did you find out about the agency?

Carol _____.

Roger Where is the agency's office?

Carol _____.

Roger Who did you see at the agency?

Carol _____.

Roger What did he ask you?

Carol _____.

Roger Did he say anything about you?

Carol _____.

Roger Did he say anything about his other models?

Carol _____.

Roger How much did you have to pay?

Carol _____.

Roger What did Mr O'Brien say you would get for your money?

Carol _____.

Roger What has happened since your interview?

Carol _____ .

Roger What happened when you telephoned?

Carol _____.

Roger What happened when you asked for your money back?

Carol _____.

Roger Thank you, Carol.

2 Carol had two conversations with Mr O'Brien. Use her letter to reconstruct the conversations. Role-play your conversations.

3 Roger Dunn received more letters about the *Top Girls* model agency. Look at the things Mr O'Brien said. What did the girls say in their letters?

Example

'I will make you a top model.'
He said he would make me a top model.

'You are one of the most attractive girls I have ever seen.'
'I have trained at least fifty of the best-paid models in Britain.'
'I will introduce you to the most important people in the fashion world.'
'You can earn £1,000 a week as a model.'
'You will have beautiful clothes.'
'You will travel to a lot of other countries.'
'I have one of the best photographers in the country.'
'Many of my models have expensive cars.'
'My models appear on TV.'
'You have a perfect face.'

4 If you were Roger Dunn, what would you do? Would you go and see Mr O'Brien? What questions would you ask him?

5 🎧 11 Roger Dunn decided to go to the agency.

a Listen to what happened.

b Listen again and note down what questions Roger Dunn asked.

c Role-play the interview between Roger Dunn and Mr O'Brien.

6 The producer decided to do a report about the *Top Girls* model agency in the 'Troubleshooter' programme. He has allowed Roger Dunn 5 minutes for the report. Use all the information you have from Carol's letter and Roger Dunn's interview to make the 5-minute report.

Pronunciation practice
'o' and 'a'

a 🎧 12 Listen and put the words in the correct column:

model	**pass**port	**Pat**rick	**law**yer

want	programme	Australia
jaywalking	called	father
van	wallet	court
Carlson	Paris	officer
always	report	charge
gram	parcel	smart
because		

b 🎧 13 Listen and check your answers.

c Listen again and repeat.

Well, Matt was lucky. The drug smugglers were sent to prison. The judge told Matt to be more careful. Bye.

Your life ⬇

You are a reporter on the 'Troubleshooter' programme. Make a 5-minute report about another case of injustice.

UNIT 6

ANDY

1
Hello. Remember me? I'm Andy. I started Canterbury Holidays with my sister Sue. I've always liked Geography. I like learning about other parts of the world.
I often dream about sailing to a desert island.

1 Paradise Island

🎧 2

*Wouldn't it be
    wonderful
To live on a tropical
    island
Just like Robinson
    Crusoe?
If I had enough
    money,
I'd buy an island
    in the Pacific.
I'd swim in the
    warm water.
I'd catch fish among
    the coral reefs
And cook it on a fire
On the beach.
I'd build a grass hut
And I'd sleep on the
    beach
Under the stars.
There would be no noise
    on my island
Except the sound of
    the sea
And the palm trees.
I wouldn't have to
    work.
I would be able to
    lie on the beach
And sunbathe
All day.
In fact I would
    be able to do
Exactly what
    I wanted.*

B·W

🎧 3

> But what is life really like there?

Information for volunteers coming to the South Sea Islands

There is no electricity on many of the islands, so don't bring a TV, stereo or electrical kitchen equipment. Bring a radio and a cassette recorder, but make sure that you have enough batteries.

There is no hospital. In an emergency you would have to fly to Australia, which is 1,000 miles away.

Take plenty of medicine with you, especially insect repellent, suntan cream, anti-malaria tablets and something for stomach upsets. You will have to boil and sterilize all your drinking water. Diarrhoea is a constant problem.

Food is very expensive because most of it is imported. Only a few vegetables grow on the islands and there are no animals, except for a few snakes. There are plenty of fish in the sea but there are sharks there, too!

Life can be boring on the islands. If you get bored easily, then you should not go to live on the islands. Bring a lot of books, some tools and a musical instrument.

Be very careful if you go swimming or sunbathing. You can get sunburnt very easily and you can get bitten or stung by the insects which live in the sand. Storms can start very suddenly, too, although hurricanes usually happen only in the spring and autumn.

Exercises

1 Right, wrong or don't know?

	R	W	D
a) All the islands have electricity.	☐	☐	☐
b) There is a hospital on one of the larger islands.	☐	☐	☐
c) There are mosquitoes on the islands.	☐	☐	☐
d) It is easy to get sunburnt on the islands.	☐	☐	☐
e) There is no cinema on the islands.	☐	☐	☐
f) The islands produce most of their own food.	☐	☐	☐
g) It is dangerous to swim in the sea around the islands.	☐	☐	☐
h) People get bored easily because there is nothing to do.	☐	☐	☐
i) The weather is always very calm.	☐	☐	☐

2 Organize the information into **for** and **against**.

for	**against**
sunbathe all day	*get sunburnt easily*

Can you think of any other arguments for or against life on a tropical island? Add them to your lists.

3

Language spot 1

expressing possibility

What are the reasons *for* living on a tropical island?
Use the table below to give your answers.

If I lived on a tropical island, I	would _____. would be able to _____. wouldn't have to _____.

What are the reasons *against* living on a tropical island?
Use the table below to give your answers.

If you lived on a tropical island, you	would _____. wouldn't be able to _____. would have to _____.

4 🎧4 Listen. Say what you **wouldn't have to do** or **wouldn't be able to do** on a desert island.

Example

At home I have to go to school.
But I wouldn't have to go to school there.

At home I can watch TV.
But I wouldn't be able to watch TV there.

5

Language spot 2

expressing possible dangers

Look at this picture. What possible dangers can you see?
Use the expressions in the table to help you.

You	**might could**	get	scratched bitten sunburnt cut burnt stung	by _____.

You	**might could**	cut scratch burn	yourself on _____.

6 Look at these medicines. What are they for?

Make dialogues that you might have in a chemist shop.

Example

A *Good morning. Can I help you?*
B *Have you got anything for sunburn?*
A *Yes. Here you are. Caladryl. That's £1.59, please.*

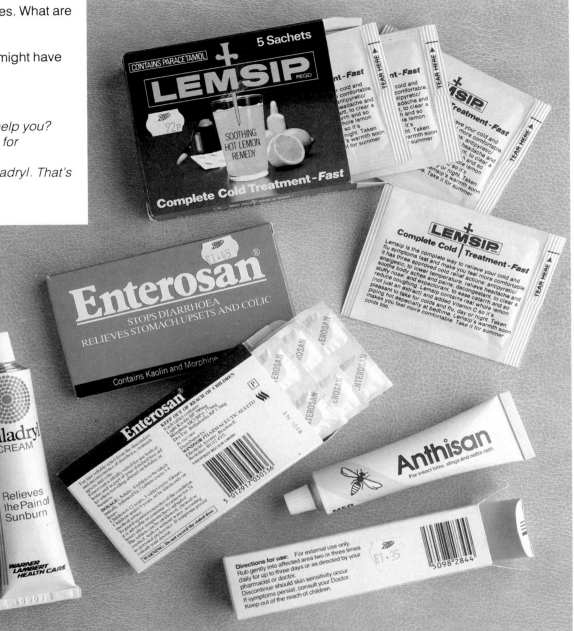

7 'Desert Island'

🎧 **5** Here is part of a radio programme called 'Desert Island'. A famous person is talking about what he would take to a desert island. Listen and complete the chart.

Question	What?	Why?
What book would you take?	'Robinson Crusoe'	helpful; learn how to cook and fish

Your life ↓

1 What do people in your class think about life on a tropical island? What would they miss most? What would they take with them? Why?

2 Make your own 'Desert Island' programme.

2 The argument

Exercises

1 Matt wasn't with the group on this trip. Andy is talking to him on the telephone now. Complete the dialogue by giving Andy's answers to Matt's questions.

Andy *Matt, there was a big argument today when Bruce came into the hut.*

Matt's questions:
Matt What were you doing, when he came in?
Andy ____
Matt Why was Bruce angry?
Andy ____
Matt What has the weather been like this week?
Andy ____
Matt How did the argument between Bruce and Sue start?
Andy ____
Matt What did Sue do?
Andy ____
Matt That wasn't very clever. What did Bruce do then?
Andy ____
Matt What was he going to do with it?
Andy ____
Matt What happened then?
Andy ____
Matt What happened after Bruce had left?
Andy ____
Matt Where is Bruce now?
Andy ____

Andy's answers:
Bruce sat on Sue's bed and made it wet. This led to an argument. We had agreed that the girls would sleep in the hut. Bruce said that he was going to sleep in the hut from now on. **(1)**
I don't know. We haven't seen him since then. **(2)**
The plate was hot and Bruce burnt his hand. He left the hut. **(3)**
We were waiting for breakfast. **(4)**
Sue started to pack her things. She called Bruce a pig-headed Aussie. **(5)**
Nina told Sue it was her fault and she started crying. **(6)**
I think he was going to throw it at Sue. **(7)**
He was freezing and he said his feet were like ice. **(8)**
He got very angry and he picked up a plate. **(9)**
The weather has been very bad this week. So far we've had thunderstorms, frost, fog, snow, hail, wind and rain. **(10)**

2a What do you think about the argument? Who was right?

b What do you think will happen? Make an ending for the story.

C Role-play the whole incident.

3

Language spot 1

describing the weather

Match the names with the symbols:

rain   snow   wind   thunderstorms
sunshine   clouds   hot weather
freezing temperatures   frost   fog

4 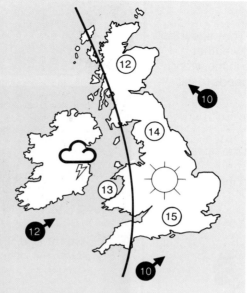 Look at these three weather maps. They show the weather for Wednesday, Thursday and Friday. Listen to the weather forecast and label the maps with the correct day.

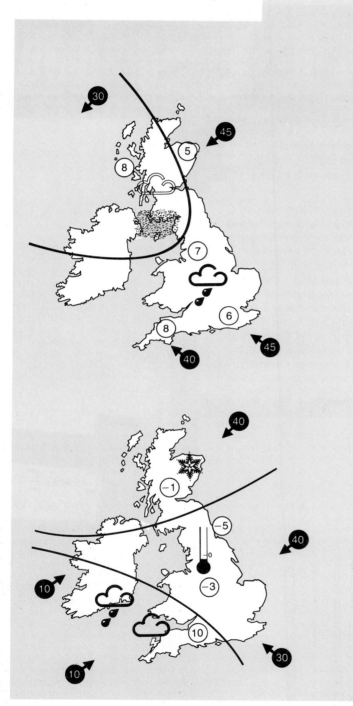

5

Language spot 2

weather forecasts

a Listen to the weather forecasts again and complete the tables with these words:

snow   cold   cloudy   rain   windy   fog   wet

It	's going to will	be	sunny. ————. ————. foggy. fine. ————. warm. ————. dry.
It	's going to will		————. rain.

There	's going to will	be	some	thunderstorms. ————. snow. ————

b Look at the maps and say what the symbols mean.

Example

This means it's going to rain.

6 Film speeds

Look at these pictures. They show the film speeds for different weather conditions. But they are in the wrong order. Match the film speeds to the correct diagram.

Clues:

1 The brighter the light the faster the speed.
2 The slower the speed the lower the *F* number.

| F16 | F11 | F8 | F5.6 | F4 | F2.8 |

Your life ↓

Make the weather forecast for your country. Say what the weather has been like today and what it will be like tomorrow.

3 Trees in danger

∩ 8

TREES IN

Millions of years before animals lived on land, there were trees on the Earth. But today trees are in serious danger.

In the 1970s, many of the elm trees in Europe were killed by Dutch elm disease. Now an even greater danger is threatening the forests and woods of Europe from northern Sweden to southern Italy. This new danger attacks all trees – deciduous trees like oak, beech and birch as well as coniferous trees like fir and pine. First the branches turn yellow and brown. Then the trees' needles or leaves fall. The roots and the trunk shrink. Finally the trees die. In the Black Forest in southern Germany 75% of the trees have been damaged or killed.

STOP ACID RAIN

CLEANER ENERGY
STOP ACID RAIN

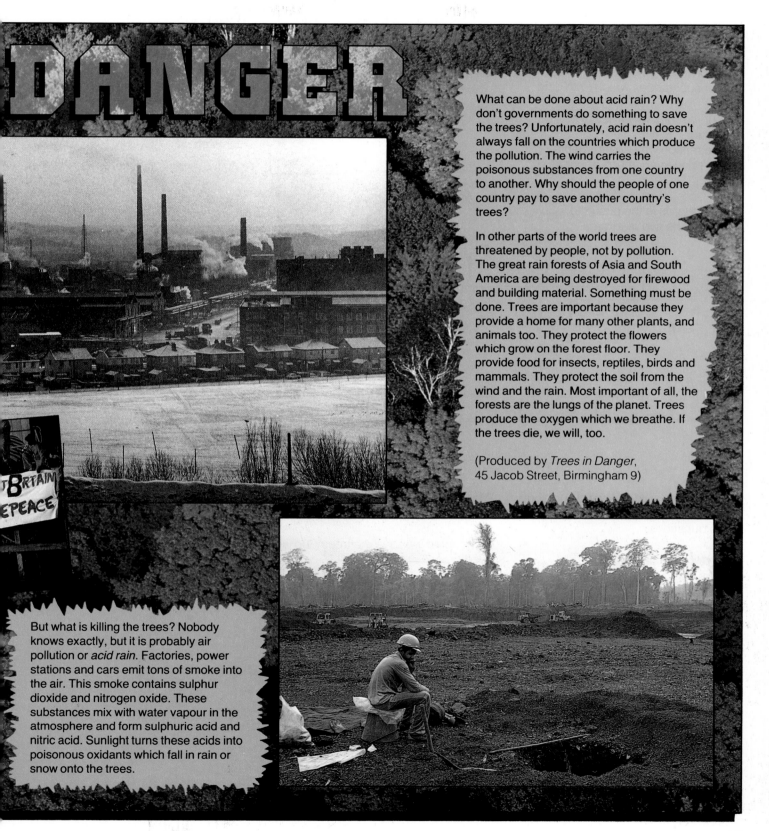

DANGER

What can be done about acid rain? Why don't governments do something to save the trees? Unfortunately, acid rain doesn't always fall on the countries which produce the pollution. The wind carries the poisonous substances from one country to another. Why should the people of one country pay to save another country's trees?

In other parts of the world trees are threatened by people, not by pollution. The great rain forests of Asia and South America are being destroyed for firewood and building material. Something must be done. Trees are important because they provide a home for many other plants, and animals too. They protect the flowers which grow on the forest floor. They provide food for insects, reptiles, birds and mammals. They protect the soil from the wind and the rain. Most important of all, the forests are the lungs of the planet. Trees produce the oxygen which we breathe. If the trees die, we will, too.

(Produced by *Trees in Danger*, 45 Jacob Street, Birmingham 9)

But what is killing the trees? Nobody knows exactly, but it is probably air pollution or *acid rain*. Factories, power stations and cars emit tons of smoke into the air. This smoke contains sulphur dioxide and nitrogen oxide. These substances mix with water vapour in the atmosphere and form sulphuric acid and nitric acid. Sunlight turns these acids into poisonous oxidants which fall in rain or snow onto the trees.

Exercises

1a Read the poster and find:

— three dangers to trees
— six kinds of tree
— four kinds of animal
— three things which produce air pollution
— four substances which form acid rain
— four reasons why trees are important
— one reason why governments haven't done very much about acid rain

b Find words in the poster to complete the two diagrams.

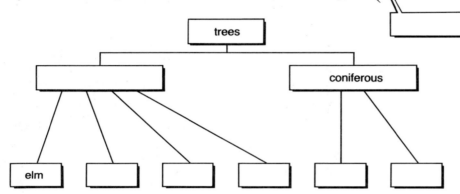

4

Language spot 1

the passive

Many trees **are killed by** disease. Now the forests **are threatened by** a greater danger.

Use the **passive** to complete these sentences:

Example

Sulphur dioxide and nitrogen oxide/emit/factories, power stations and cars

*Sulphur dioxide and nitrogen oxide **are emitted by** factories, power stations and cars.*

a) Trees/damage/acid rain

b) Poisonous oxidants/drop onto trees/rain and snow

c) Sulphur dioxide and nitrogen oxide/turn into sulphuric acid and nitric acid/water vapour

d) Forests/destroy

e) Sulphuric acid and nitric acid/turn into poisonous oxidants/sunlight

f) Pollution/blow from one country to another/wind

2 A reporter is interviewing someone from *Trees in Danger*. Give answers to the questions.

Reporter's questions:
What is killing the trees in Europe?

———.

Is this only in one part of Europe?

———.

How many trees have been damaged?

———.

Is acid rain like Dutch elm disease? I mean, does it damage only one kind of tree?

———.

What happens to a tree when it is affected by acid rain?

———.

How is acid rain caused?

Why don't governments do something to control acid rain?

———.

Why should we save the trees? Do we need them?

———.

3 What do you think should be done?
Write down five things which governments and people should do to save the trees.

Q What did the daddy chimney say to the boy chimney?
A You're too young to smoke.

5 Look at this diagram. It shows how acid rain is produced. Use your sentences from *Exercise 4* to label the diagram.

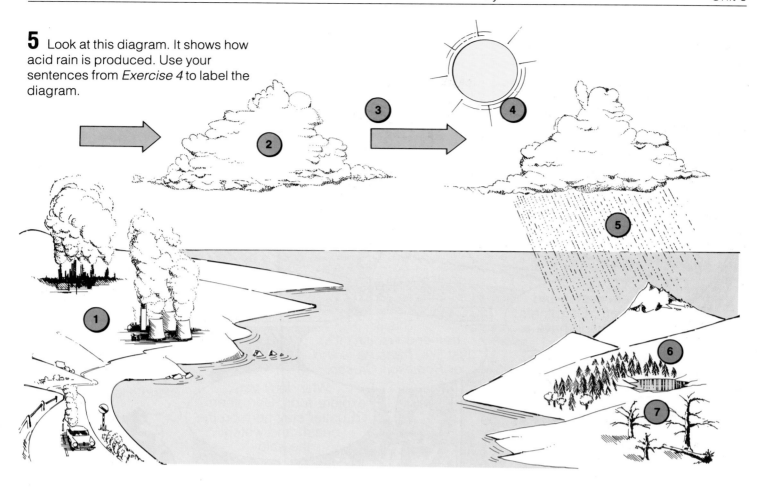

6

Language spot 2

classifying

a Put these plants, animals, birds, etc. into the correct columns.

tree	reptile	mammal	bird	insect	fish

snake ostrich elm butterfly pelican whale shark
oak parrot lion mouse dolphin pine lizard
fly owl fir crocodile pigeon eagle tortoise birch

b Ask and answer.

Example

A *What is a birch?*
B *It's a kind of tree.*

Boy Ouch, a crab just bit my toe.
Girl Which one?
Boy I don't know. All crabs look the same to me.

Pollution

Pollution affects many things: buildings, rivers, animals, the air which we breathe, the sea.

1 Find out about how pollution is affecting your town or your country.

2 Make a poster about the problem.

Exercises

1 Carruthers' diary

Can you complete it?

> We have left ____ and we have got jobs as waiters on a small ____ which is sailing across the ____ ____—to America.
> Today we had a lifeboat ____. We put on our ____ ____ and we got into the ____. While we were in the lifeboat, we saw an ____. We went to have a ____ at it. We ____ to the Island. Carstairs said that he would ____ and watch the ship, while I ____ the island.
> When I got back to the ____, Carstairs was ____ and our boat had ____. Carstairs panicked. He thought we were ____ on the Island. I wish I ____ read ____

2

3

Language spot 2

expressing regret

We **should have** stayed near the ship.
We **shouldn't have** left the ship.

Use the cues in *Exercise 2* and say what
they should or shouldn't have done.

4 🎧 **10** Listen. Complete what
Carstairs is saying with **should** or
shouldn't have. Use the cues in
Exercise 2 to help you.

Example

Oh no! It's raining now. We're going to
get wet.
We should have built a hut.

5 Look at these tools. Which ones
would you take to a desert island?
You can take only three.

Your life ↓

Marooned

You are marooned. Write a short
play about it.

1 Decide where you are
marooned: up a mountain, in a
boat at sea, on an island?

2 Decide how you got there.

3 Decide what you would do.

4 Write and act your play.

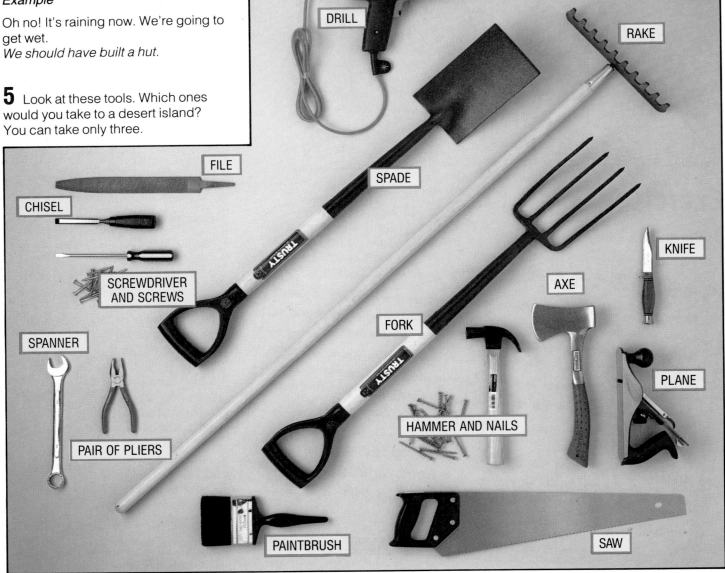

5 | **Maps**

🎧 11

Exercises

1 Look at this picture for 1 minute. Then work in pairs. One student closes the book, the other asks questions.

Example

Are the mountains to the west of the swamp?
Is the jungle to the south of the river?
Are the mountains in the northern part of the island?

2

Language spot 1

compass points

Complete the chart:

noun	adjective
north	northern
south	_____
_____	eastern
west	_____
north-west	north-western
south-west	_____
north-east	_____
_____	south-eastern

3 Here is a map of the part of the island where Carstairs and Carruthers landed. On the first four days they explored the island. Here are the four reports. Can you draw the complete map of the island?

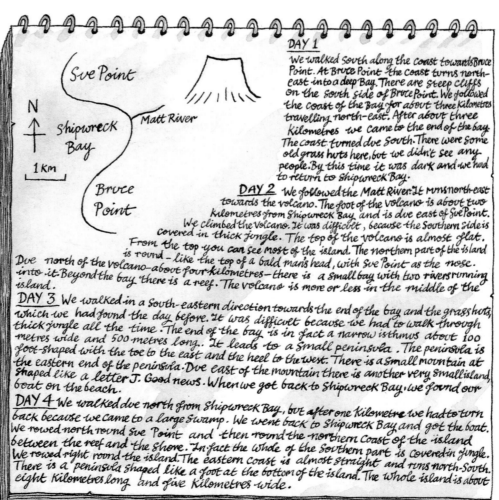

DAY 1 We walked south along the coast towards Bruce Point. At Bruce Point the coast turns north-east into a deep Bay. There are steep cliffs on the south side of Bruce Point. We followed the coast of the Bay for about three kilometres travelling north-east. After about three kilometres we came to the end of the bay. The coast turned due south. There were some old grass huts here, but we didn't see any people. By this time it was dark and we had to return to Shipwreck Bay.

DAY 2 We followed the Matt River. It runs north-east towards the volcano. The foot of the volcano is about two kilometres from Shipwreck Bay and is due east of Sue Point. We climbed the volcano. It was difficult, because the southern side is covered in thick jungle. The top of the volcano is almost flat. From the top you can see most of the island. The northern part of the island is round – like the top of a bald man's head, with Sue Point as the nose. Due north of the volcano – about four kilometres – there is a small bay with two rivers running into it. Beyond the bay there is a reef. The volcano is more or less in the middle of the island.

DAY 3 We walked in a south-eastern direction towards the end of the bay and the grass huts, which we had found the day before. It was difficult because we had to walk through thick jungle all the time. The end of the bay is in fact a narrow isthmus about 100 metres wide and 500 metres long. It leads to a small peninsula. The peninsula is foot-shaped with the toe to the east and the heel to the west. There is a small mountain at the eastern end of the peninsula. Due east of the mountain there is another very small island, shaped like a letter J. Good news. When we got back to Shipwreck Bay, we found our boat on the beach.

DAY 4 We walked due north from Shipwreck Bay, but after one kilometre we had to turn back because we came to a large swamp. We went back to Shipwreck Bay and got the boat. We rowed north round Sue Point and then round the northern coast of the island between the reef and the shore. In fact the whole of the southern part is covered in jungle. We rowed right round the island. The eastern coast is almost straight and runs north-south. There is a peninsula shaped like a foot at the bottom of the island. The whole island is about eight kilometres long and five kilometres wide.

4

Language spot 2

describing shapes

In the reports above find another expression which means the same as:

It's shaped like a foot.
It's ____ – ____ .

Describe these things.

Example

a heart-shaped card

5

Language spot 3

positions

Look at this diagram. Copy it and label it with these words:

side   bottom   top   middle

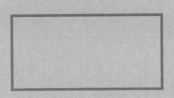

6 🔊 12 Listen and draw the shapes.

Example

The bottom of this shape is round. The left side is straight and the right side is shaped like a nose. The top is flat. In the middle of the shape, there is a star shape.

7 Draw a shape and describe it to your partner. He/she must draw what you describe.

Your life ↓

1 Draw an island.

2 Write a description of your island.

3 Give your description to another group. They must try to draw your island.

4 Compare the two drawings.

Pronunciation practice

'th' and 's'

a 🔊 13 Listen and put the words in the correct column:

thought	this	sea	desert

something
sunbathe
thunderstorms
weather
southern
south
threaten
breathe
isthmus

thick
Carruthers

sister
noise
insect
peninsula
easily
music

mosquito
reasonable
atmosphere
tortoise
disease
poisonous
asleep
Crusoe

b 🔊 14 Listen and check your answers.

c Listen again and repeat.

d Say this: **The sixth sick sheikh's sixth sheep's sick.**

UNIT 7

MATT

Hi. I'm Matt Swanson. I'm studying Medicine in England but I come from Canada.

81

1 Canada

What do you know about Canada?
Here is a short quiz. Choose the
correct answers. (There may be more
than one correct answer.)

1 The national language of Canada is

a) French ☐
b) English ☐
c) German ☐

2 The capital of Canada is

a) Montreal ☐
b) Toronto ☐
c) Ottawa ☐

3 Canada's largest city is

a) Montreal ☐
b) Toronto ☐
c) Ottawa ☐

4 Canada is

a) the largest country in the world ☐
b) the second largest country in the world ☐
c) the third largest country in the world ☐

5 The Canadian head of state is

a) the Queen ☐
b) the President ☐
c) the Prime Minister ☐

6 The national currency of Canada is

a) the Canadian pound ☐
b) the Canadian dollar ☐
c) the Canadian franc ☐

7 Canada is the world's largest producer of

a) gold ☐
b) oil ☐
c) nickel ☐

8 The ancestors of most Canadians came from

a) Britain ☐
b) Ireland ☐
c) France ☐

9 Canada's original inhabitants were

a) Eskimos ☐
b) Indians ☐
c) Japanese ☐

10 The longest river in Canada is

a) the St Lawrence ☐
b) the Mackenzie ☐
c) the Mississippi ☐

Exercises

1 Check your answers in this text.

🎧2 Canada is the largest country in the American continent and the second largest country in the world. It has a population of 24 million in an area of 9,976,185 square kilometres. Most of the population are descended from European immigrants: 45% from British and Irish ancestors, 29% from French ancestors, 6% from German ancestors. Only 1.5% of today's population are descended from the original Eskimo and Indian inhabitants.

Britain and France fought over Canada for nearly two hundred years. Finally in 1763 Britain took control. Canada is now an independent country with its own prime minister, but the head of state is still the British Queen.

Canada is a bilingual country. The majority of the population speak English. Most French speakers live in the province of Quebec. Canada's largest city, Montreal, is in Quebec. It has a population of 2,720,413. But Montreal is not the capital city. The capital is Ottawa in the province of Ontario.

The national emblem of Canada is the maple leaf and the currency is the Canadian dollar.

2 Copy this chart and complete it with information from the text in *Exercise 1*.

Name:	
Area:	
Population:	
Language(s):	
Capital:	
Largest city:	
Head of State:	
Head of Government:	
Currency:	
National emblem:	
Longest river:	
Main products:	
industry:	
minerals:	
forestry:	
agriculture:	

Canada is a huge country. Its longest river, the Mackenzie, flows for 1,600 km into the Arctic Ocean. It is also a very rich country. It has many industries (cars, electrical goods, etc.). It produces almost every mineral (gold, silver, iron, copper, uranium, oil, coal, etc.). Canada is the world's biggest producer of nickel, the second biggest producer of zinc and the third biggest producer of lead. Canada is also one of the world's biggest producers of wood and paper (44% of the land is forest). Agriculture (mostly wheat and cattle) is important, too.

3 Copy and complete this pie graph about the population of Canada.

The ancestors of Canada's population

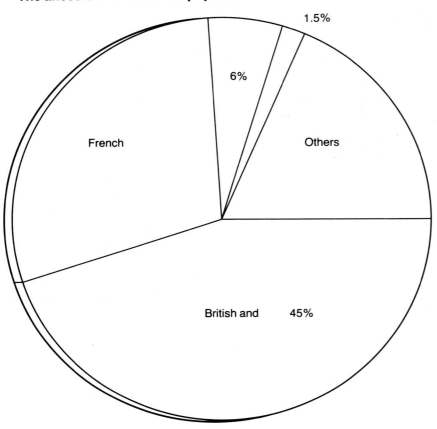

1.5%

6%

French

Others

British and   45%

4

Language spot 1

large numbers

2,675,891 = two million, six hundred and seventy-five thousand, eight hundred and ninety-one

406,873,241 = four hundred and six million, eight hundred and seventy-three thousand, two hundred and forty-one

Say these in full:

387,764,034
98,562,607
6,541,987,000
87,000,000
78,000,000,000

5 World population

Which areas of the world have the biggest populations?

a Put these in the correct order:

North America
Europe
Oceania (Australia, New Zealand and the Pacific islands)
Asia (including the USSR)
Africa
South America

b 🎧3 Listen and write down the population of each area.

6

Language spot 2

percentages

a Fill in the missing items:

45% ____ the population have ____ or Irish ancestors.
____ of the population have French ____.
1.5% of the population have ____ or ____ ancestors.

b You know the total population of Canada and the percentages. How many people are there in each group?

c Look at your answers to *Exercise 5b*. What percentage of the world's population lives in each area?

d Make a pie graph to show the distribution of the world's population.

7 Look at the information about Canada in *Exercise 2*. Make another chart like this and fill it in with the details of your own country.

Use the information in your chart. Write a simple introduction to your country. Illustrate it with maps and pictures.

2 First aid

FRACTURES AND SPRAINS
🎧4 **WHAT TO DO**

If someone has hurt a limb:

- it will be painful.
- they might not be able to move it.
- it might be swollen.
- it might be discoloured.
- the person may be in a state of shock.

It is difficult to tell a fracture from a sprain, so the patient ought to have an X-ray.

What should you do?

An injured leg:

Don't move the limb.

Cover the patient with a blanket.

Send for help. Phone the doctor or dial 999 for an ambulance.

If you have to move the patient, carry him or her on a stretcher.

Don't give the patient anything to drink.

An injured arm, wrist or hand:

Support the arm in a sling.

Put a blanket around the patient's shoulders.

Take the patient to a doctor or to a hospital.

A cut:

If the patient has cut himself or herself, you should try to stop the bleeding. Hold the edges of the cut together. (Make sure your hands are clean!)

If possible, put a bandage or a plaster on the wound. (Make sure it isn't too tight.)

If the wound is dirty, the patient might need an anti-tetanus injection. Take the patient to a doctor or hospital.

Exercises

1 Match the instructions with the correct pictures.

a) Put a bandage on the wound.
b) Support the arm in a sling.
c) Don't give the patient anything to drink.
d) Take the patient to a doctor or to a hospital.
e) Put a blanket round the patient's shoulders.
f) Don't move the limb. Cover the patient with a blanket.
g) Have an anti-tetanus injection.
h) Send for help.
i) Make sure your hands are clean!
j) Make sure the bandage isn't too tight.
k) Hold the edges of the cut together.

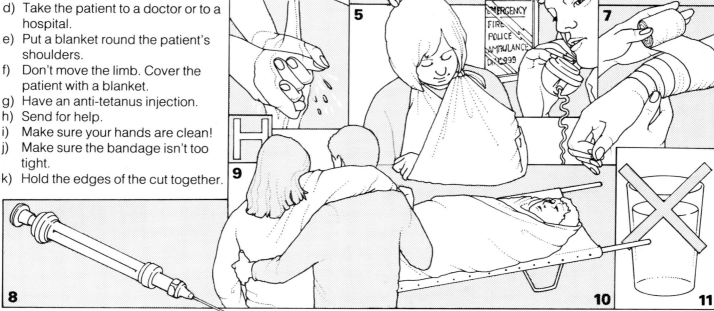

2 Find words in the text which mean the same as:

an arm or leg
a broken bone
someone who has hurt himself/herself
  or needs medical attention
a cut
hurt
bigger than normal
not a normal colour

3 What **should** and **shouldn't** you do in these cases?

a)

I've hurt my wrist.

b)

I think I've broken my leg.

Is it cut?

Yes.

c)

She's cut her arm and I think it's broken, too.

Example

(for **a**)

You should support the arm in a sling.
You shouldn't move your wrist.

Patient Doctor, doctor, everybody thinks I'm a liar.
Doctor I don't believe you.

4

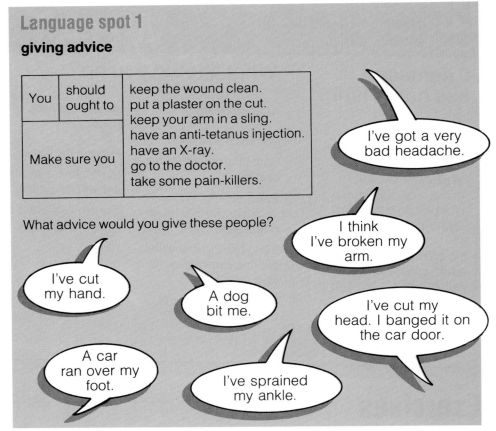

Language spot 1

giving advice

You	should ought to	keep the wound clean. put a plaster on the cut. keep your arm in a sling.
Make sure you		have an anti-tetanus injection. have an X-ray. go to the doctor. take some pain-killers.

What advice would you give these people?

I've got a very bad headache.

I think I've broken my arm.

I've cut my hand.

A dog bit me.

I've cut my head. I banged it on the car door.

A car ran over my foot.

I've sprained my ankle.

5 **At the doctor's**

a 🎧 **5** Listen to these interviews between a doctor and her patients. Complete a form for each patient.

b Role-play the conversations.

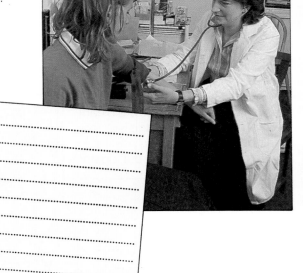

Patient: ....
....
Problem: ....
....
Diagnosis: ....
....
Treatment: ....
....
....

6

Language spot 2

expressing frequency

In the doctor's conversation in *Exercise 5* find
another way of saying these:

Take the medicine	twice a day (x2 pd)
	four times a day (x4 pd)

Say these in both ways:
x6 pd
x2 pd
x8 pd
x1 pd (note: once a day)
x3 pd

Your life ↓

You are going to a tropical island.
What would you take in a first aid
kit? Why would you take each
item?

7 Here are some more forms. Make
the conversations with the doctor.
Role-play your conversations.

Patient: Philip Hall
Problem: Sore eye
Diagnosis: infection
Treatment: eye drops x4 pd

Patient: Christina Williams
Problem: painful elbow
Diagnosis: sprain
Treatment: crepe bandage / sling

Patient: Julia Bevan
Problem: cut finger
Diagnosis: --------
Treatment: bandage
anti-tetanus
antibiotics x3 pd

Patient: David Stewart
Problem: painful foot
Diagnosis: broken toe
Treatment: X-ray
pain killers x2 pd

That's funny. He's fainted. Perhaps he thought I was the ghost behind the curtain. How silly. I don't believe in ghosts.

Question Why do witches ride on brooms?
Answer Vacuum cleaners are too heavy.

Exercises

1 Right, wrong or don't know?

		R	W	D
a	Carstairs and Carruthers are in New York.	☐	☐	☐
b)	They can't find a hotel room.	☐	☐	☐
c)	The hotel is haunted by the ghost of an old woman.	☐	☐	☐
d)	She was very poor.	☐	☐	☐
e)	She used to count her money every twelve hours.	☐	☐	☐
f)	The old woman hadn't looked after the house very well.	☐	☐	☐
g)	Carstairs and Carruthers didn't want to spend the night in the old house.	☐	☐	☐
h)	Carruthers got up to close the bathroom window.	☐	☐	☐
i)	Carstairs thought Carruthers was the ghost.	☐	☐	☐
j)	The story about the ghost wasn't true.	☐	☐	☐

2

Language spot 1

used to

She **used to** count her money.

a What do you think **used to** means?
– She *still* counts the money.
– She *counted* the money *regularly*.
– She *counted* the money *regularly*, *but she doesn't anymore*.
– She *counted* the money *regularly* and *she still does*.

b Say what the old woman **used to** do.

Example

live in the old house
She used to live in the old house.

eat only bread and cheese
wear old clothes
live alone
hide her money under the bed
save all her money
count her money at midnight
drive visitors away

c Look. Say what Matt **used to** do.

Example

I don't live in Canada any more.
He used to live in Canada.

I don't smoke any more.

I'm not a student now.

I haven't got a girlfriend any more.

I haven't got a car any more.

I don't live with my parents any more.

I don't play American football any more.

I'm not fat now.

3

Language spot 2

have something done

a Look at these two sentences. What is the difference?

The owner **ought to have** the window **mended**.
The owner **ought to mend** the window.

Clue: Who would do the repair?

b Here are some more things that are wrong with the house. Say what the owner **ought to have done**.

Use: repair, replace, clean, repaint, decorate

The roof has got a hole in it.
The kitchen window is broken.
The paint is coming off the doors.
The light bulb in the hall is broken.
The pipes under the sink are leaking.
The bath is cracked.
The wallpaper is coming off the walls.
The carpets are dirty.
The cushions have got holes in.
The curtains are torn.

4

The group had an accident in the van. They had to have a lot of things done to it. Look at page 23 and say what they had done.

Example

They had the puncture repaired.

5 The plumber's accident

Look at these parts of a dialogue. They show what happened to a plumber who went to a house to repair a pipe.

a 🎧8 Listen to the story. Then put the dialogue in the correct order.

b Role-play the story.

Oh, hello. Are you the plumber? It's the pipe under the sink. I'm just going out. I'll be back soon. **(1)**
Ooooooh. I think I'm going to faint. **(2)**
CRASH! Ow, my head! **(3)**
Hmmm. This is too difficult for me to do. I'll have to call a plumber. **(4)**
All right. Can you give me a hand to put him on the stretcher and carry him downstairs? Tell me, how did he hurt his head? **(5)**
Oh no! He's broken his leg and his arm now! **(6)**
Oh dear. The pipe under the sink has got a hole in it. We ought to have it repaired. **(7)**
Yes, sir. I'll come straightaway. **(8)**
We'll have to take them both to hospital now. **(9)**
Hello, darling. I'm back. I can see you under the sink. Tickle, tickle, tickle. **(10)**
Hello. Is that the plumber? Can you come and repair a pipe for me, please? **(11)**

Oh, who are you? I thought you were my husband. **(12)**
Help quickly! I need an ambulance! **(13)**
(BANG, CRASH, BANG.) Owwwwwwwwww. My leg! My arm! Owwww. **(14)**
When I came home, I saw a pair of legs under the sink. I thought it was my husband, so I tickled his stomach. He sat up too quickly and he banged his head on the sink. **(15)**
Ha ha ha. That's the funniest thing I've ever heard. Ha ha ha. **(16)**
It's all right, dear. I'll repair it. **(17)**
Oh, you are clever. I'm just going to the shops. I won't be long. **(18)**
Look out! Don't drop the stretcher! **(19)**

Make a ghost story. Role-play your story.

4 Risk

⌂9 We do some dangerous things on our journeys. Do you remember when our van almost went over the edge of the cliff? But how dangerous is travelling? What are the chances of being killed, if you just stay at home?

In this group of people number 2 is a farmworker, number 11 is a businessman. Which one is more at risk in his daily life?

The farmworker does a lot of different jobs on the farm, but he spends most of his time working with machinery, such as driving a tractor. He lives in a small village with his wife and children. He always goes to work on a motorbike. He smokes 20 cigarettes a day, but he never drinks. He regularly plays football for a local team.

The businessman sells office equipment. He frequently travels abroad and he usually goes by air. He is a non-smoker, but he drinks about a bottle of wine a day. He lives in a small town. There is a nuclear power station less than a mile from his home. His hobby is rock climbing, although he seldom has enough time for it.

Which man is more likely to meet an accidental death?

Exercises

1a Make a chart like this and complete it with information from the text:

occupation	farmworker	businessman
travel environment habits hobbies		

b Look at the information in your chart. Which activities do you think carry the greater risks?

Question What have a goat and a letter-box got in common?
Answer Neither of them can drive a tractor.

2 Read this and compare it to your own ideas.

Risk analysis

In risk analysis, you try to calculate the dangers of any activity. Let's look at the lives of the businessman and farmworker. The farmworker is in a high-risk job with a *1 in 9,000* risk of being killed at work. Most farm accidents involve machinery. So this man's risks are probably higher than average. The businessman, however, is probably safer at work than at home. His chances of being killed at work are about *100,000 to 1*. You might think that the businessman's air travel is a high risk. But in fact the risk is only *25,000 to 1*. Riding a motorcycle carries a *500 to 1* chance of being killed.

What about smoking and drinking? Here again the businessman's risk is lower. The bottle of wine a day gives a *13,000 to 1* risk, but the packet of cigarettes a day carries a *200 to 1* chance of death.

Rock climbing is certainly more dangerous than football, but it carries only a *25,000 to 1* risk.

But what about the nuclear power station? The businessman's risk here is about the same as the farmworker's risk of dying from a snakebite, i.e. *several million to 1*.

From these figures which man do you think has the more dangerous life?

3 Find words and expressions which mean the same as:

He doesn't smoke.
a very dangerous job
20 cigarettes
danger
flying
dying
motorcycle
every day
to other countries

4

Language spot 1

chances

Look at these two ways of expressing the **chances** or **risks** of doing something:

9,000 to 1
1 in 9,000

Do they mean exactly the same?

What are the chances?

What are the chances of throwing a six?

What are each runner's chances of winning?

What are the chances of finding the correct room first time?

5

Language spot 2

comparing activities

Use this table to make true sentences:

Working on a farm Selling office equipment Smoking Drinking wine Living near a nuclear power station Being bitten by a snake Driving a tractor Flying Rock climbing Riding a motorbike	is	more less	dangerous than	rock climbing. living near a nuclear power station. being bitten by a snake. working on a farm. selling office equipment. driving a tractor. flying. riding a motorbike. smoking. drinking wine.

6

Language spot 3

adverbs of frequency

a Put these adverbs in order from the *least* frequent to the *most* frequent:

often always never sometimes seldom frequently

b Use these words to say how often the two men do these things.

Example

*The farmworker **always** rides a motorbike to work.*
*The businessman **never** rides a motorbike to work.*

ride a motorbike to work
smoke
travel abroad
work in an office
drive a tractor
go rock climbing
play football
drink wine
travel by air

7

Look at the other people in the picture. Match these names to the people.

coalminer   jockey
waitress   president
skier   building worker
boxer   racing driver
farmworker   rock climber
train driver   motorcyclist
housewife   pilot
businessman

Who takes the greatest risks? For example:
Is skiing safer than boxing? Is working at home more dangerous than working in a restaurant?
Put the people in order, the person who takes the *most* risks first.

8 Listen.

a Note down the risks.

Example

Farmworker: 9,000 to 1

b Compare the table to your own list.

Pronunciation practice

stress

a Look at these words. Mark the stressed syllable:

Example

first	second	third
Canada	Ca**nad**ian	inde**pen**dent

American	producer	machinery
ancestors	agriculture	businessman
European	injection	occupation
population	ambulance	president
majority	support	pilot
Eskimo	hotel	
industry	cigarette	

b 🔊 11 Listen and check your answers.

c Find more words for each group.

Analyse your own life. Make a list of your activities. Say how often you do them. What risks are you taking in your daily life?

Take care now, and don't take too many risks. See you.

1 Stonehenge

⌂ 2 Eight miles north of Salisbury is a large circle of stones, which is called Stonehenge. Nobody knows why it was built or what it was used for.

Was it an ancient cemetery? There are many graves around the monument. Was it a kind of observatory, where astronomers studied the stars and the planets? Was it a place where witches and magicians offered human sacrifices to the gods? Or was it a temple, where the ancient Britons worshipped the Sun? The monument faces the point on the horizon where the sun rises on Midsummer's Day. We shall never know the real answer.

Work started on Stonehenge around 1800 BC, but the monument, whose ruins you can see today, was built four hundred years later, around 1400 BC.

The ruins stand in the centre of a huge circle 320 ft (98 m) in diameter. The circle is formed by a bank and a ditch. The bank is now only 2 ft (0.64 m) high, but it was probably much higher when it was built. The ditch is 7 ft (2.1 m) deep. There is a gap, 35 ft (10.7 m) wide, in the north-east side.

The ruins consist of two stone circles and two stone horseshoes. The stones in the outer circle are 16 ft (4.87 m) high and 6 ft (1.83 m) thick.

These stones were joined by a continuous line of stones, which lay on the top of the uprights. But most of these have fallen down. The stones in the inner circle are about 6 ft (1.83 m) high.

The outer horseshoe consists of five trilithons. ('Trilithon' is a Greek word, which means 'three stones'.) The tallest of these trilithons is 28 ft (8.53 m) high. In the centre of the horseshoe there is a large stone, 16 ft (4.88 m) long, called the Altar Stone.

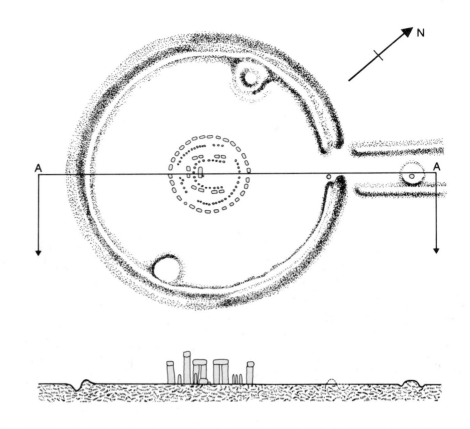

Exercises

1 A tour guide is describing Stonehenge, but a lot of it is wrong. Say what is wrong.

Stonehenge is eight miles west of Salisbury. Some people believe it was a temple, where the ancient Britons worshipped the Moon. Other people believe it was an observatory, where archaeology students studied the stars. But most people think that it was a place where astronomers offered animal sacrifices to the Sun.

Stonehenge was built in 1600 BC, but it was destroyed four hundred years later.

2a Look at these drawings. Which parts of Stonehenge do they show?

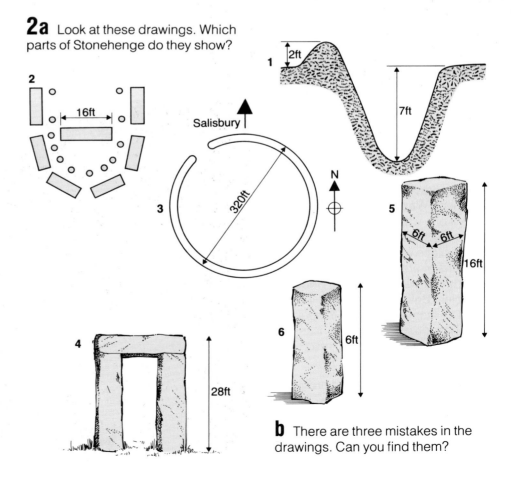

b There are three mistakes in the drawings. Can you find them?

3

Language spot 1

relative clauses with where

Stonehenge was a temple.
People worshipped the Sun at Stonehenge.
Stonehenge was a temple, **where** people worshipped
the Sun.

a Use the cues to say what people think Stonehenge
was.

Cues:

temple/people/worship the Sun
observatory/astronomers/study the stars
place/witches/make human sacrifices
cemetery/ancient Britons/bury their dead kings
palace/giants/live
temple/people/worship the stars

b Think of a place and describe it to your partner.
Your partner must guess what the place is.

Example

A *This is a place in a house where you sleep.*
B *It's a bedroom.*

4

Language spot 2

shapes

Find words in the text to describe the other shapes.

a _____   a rectangle   a square

a triangle   a _____   a diamond

5

Language spot 3

dimensions

What are the missing words?

Example

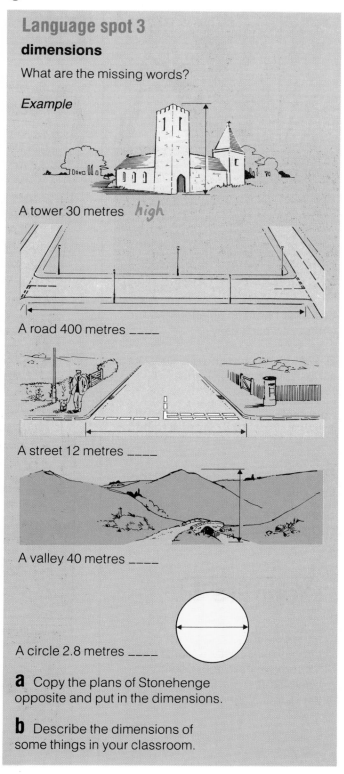

A tower 30 metres *high*

A road 400 metres _____

A street 12 metres _____

A valley 40 metres _____

A circle 2.8 metres _____

a Copy the plans of Stonehenge
opposite and put in the dimensions.

b Describe the dimensions of
some things in your classroom.

6 Draw a shape and describe it to
your partner. Your partner must draw
what you describe. Compare the two
drawings.

7 Endurance course

Last year I went on an endurance course. It wasn't easy.

a 🎧 3 Listen and find out what I had to do. Complete the chart.

obstacle	dimensions

b Describe what Cindy had to do on the course.

Some words to help you:
crawl, obstacle, muddy

Your life ↓

Most countries have some famous ruins. Write a tourist guide for some ruins in your country. Use pictures, diagrams and maps to illustrate your guidebook.

2 Carstairs and Carruthers 🎧 4

Exercises

1a Look at Carruthers' diary. Make his conversation with the captain.

b Make an ending for the story.

2 The end

Put together all the parts of the story from when Carruthers and Carstairs arrived in England. Role-play the story.

Start like this:

Carruthers Well. Here we are, Carstairs. Back in dear old England. And we're home in time for Christmas. I'll just pack my suitcase . . .

3

Language spot 1

question tags

Look back at *all* the Carstairs and Carruthers stories and make a quiz of ten questions. Then ask and answer the questions.

Example

A *Where was Carstairs put in prison?*

B *It was in Australia, wasn't it?*

What should Carruthers do with the money? What would you do? Would you share it with Carstairs?

4

Language spot 2

dates and festivals 🎧6

a Write the names of the months in full.

b Read the dates in the list. Remember: *Jan 22 = January the twenty-second.*

c Make a list of public holidays in England and in Scotland. What are the differences?

This diary belongs to:

Cindy Cass

Important dates (★ = Public holiday)

★ New Year's Day	Jan 1
★ Holiday (Scotland only)	Jan 2
St Valentine's Day	Feb 14
St David's Day	Mar 1
Mother's Day	Mar 9
St Patrick's Day	Mar 17
★ Good Friday	Mar 28
★ Easter Monday (not Scotland)	Mar 31
St George's Day	Apr 23
★ May Day Holiday	May 5
★ Spring Holiday	May 26
★ Holiday (Scotland only)	Aug 4
★ August Bank Holiday (not Scotland)	Aug 25
St Andrew's Day	Nov 30
Christmas Eve	Dec 24
★ Christmas Day	Dec 25
★ Boxing Day (not Scotland)	Dec 26
New Year's Eve	Dec 31

Personal dates to remember:

My birthday	*Feb 9*
Mum's birthday	*June 17*
Dad's birthday	*July 20*
Ken's birthday	*Oct 3*
Mum and Dad's wedding anniversary	*Sept 15*

5

Look at these cards which Cindy and her family received. Match them to the postmarks:

6 A game: Happy Birthday, Mum

Look at Cindy's diary again.
A chooses a date.
B gives the appropriate greeting.

Example

A *June 17.*
B *Happy Birthday, Mum.*

Your life ↓

Make a list of the important dates in your year. Include public and personal dates.

🎧 7 I was away from home last Christmas for the first time. My Mum wrote to me. Here's her letter.

45 Caledonian Road
Leeds
Yorkshire
24ᵗʰ December 1986

Dear Cindy,

It's Christmas Eve and as usual the house is full of people and noise. I've got the vegetables and the Christmas Pudding ready for tomorrow's dinner. Your Dad is in the kitchen now. He's preparing the turkey, so there won't be much to do tomorrow morning. I'm going to church in the morning, after we've opened the presents. I love singing the carols on Christmas Day.

Ken and Sarah arrived on the 22ⁿᵈ with the children. Dan and Jenny are very excited. Dan says he wants a big lorry from Father Christmas and Jenny wants a doll. They sat at the window waiting to see the reindeer and the sleigh. I told them that Father Christmas wouldn't come till they were asleep. Jenny was very worried yesterday afternoon, because we haven't got a chimney. She wanted to know how Father Christmas would get down. They're in bed now, but I'm sure they'll be awake early in the morning. Ken's putting their presents in their pillow cases now. Some of the toys are so big nowadays. I can remember when I was a girl, we used to hang up a stocking for our presents. A stocking certainly wouldn't be big enough for today's toys. And yet kids still talk about hanging up a stocking. Funny, isn't it?

Sarah has made a beautiful Christmas cake for tea tomorrow. We had a bit of a problem with the Christmas tree. Your Dad was putting the decorations on it yesterday. While he was fixing the angel to the top of the tree, it fell over and landed on the cat. The tree is all right now and it looks lovely with the lights on it and the presents underneath it. The cat hasn't been near the tree since.

On Boxing Day the neighbours are coming in. In the afternoon your Dad and Ken are going to the football match. Sarah is visiting some friends. I think I'll just have a rest and watch TV.

We all hope that you are well. We miss you very much and we wish you could be with us at Christmas.

All our love,

Mum and Dad. ✗✗

1 Christmas is the most important festival in England and there are a lot of Christmas traditions. Read Cindy's letter from her parents and find the answers to these questions about Christmas traditions in England.

a) What do people put on their Christmas tree?
b) When do people open their presents?
c) Who brings the children's presents?
d) When does he bring them?
e) How does he deliver them?
f) What do children hang up for their presents?
g) What is the traditional food for dinner on Christmas Day?
h) What is the traditional food for tea on Christmas Day?
i) What do people do on Boxing Day?
j) What are the traditional Christmas hymns called?

2 How many of the things mentioned in the letter can you find in pictures?

3

Language spot 1

time prepositions: in, on, at

a Find the correct prepositions for these:

in, **on** or **at**

Christmas Eve
Christmas
the twentieth century
December 26
the morning
Wednesday
1987
nine o'clock
January

b Now make a rule. Which preposition do you use? for:

– days
– parts of the day
– years
– times of day
– centuries
– festivals
– months

4

🎧 **8** Read Cindy's letter again. Listen to these conversations. When did they happen?

Example

on 23rd December in the afternoon

5

Language spot 2

the present continuous with future meaning

Fill in the missing verbs.

Tomorrow morning I ____ ____ to church.
On Boxing Day the neighbours ____ ____ in.
In the afternoon your Dad and Ken ____ ____ to the football match.
On Boxing Day Sarah ____ ____ some friends.

– What tense is this?
– How do we know it has a future meaning?

6

What is Andy doing next week?

Example

On Monday morning he's collecting the van from the garage.

What are you doing next week?

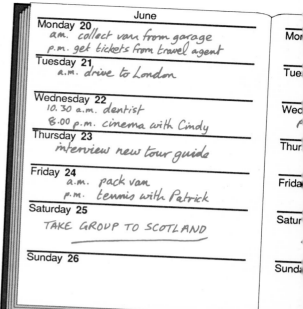

June

Monday 20
a.m. collect van from garage
p.m. get tickets from travel agent

Tuesday 21
a.m. drive to London

Wednesday 22
10.30 a.m. dentist
8.00 p.m. cinema with Cindy

Thursday 23
interview new tour guide

Friday 24
a.m. pack van
p.m. tennis with Patrick

Saturday 25
TAKE GROUP TO SCOTLAND

Sunday 26

Your life ⬇

1 Compare the English Christmas to your most important festival.

– What is the most important festival in your country?
– When is it?
– What do you do?
– Are there traditional stories about it?
– Do you eat special food?

2 Write a letter to a friend in Britain describing your most important festival.

🎧 **9** **A Christmas Carol**

God rest ye merry gentlemen

God rest ye merry
gentlemen,
Let nothing you dismay.
Remember Christ our Saviour,
Was born on Christmas day
To save us all from Satan's
power,
When we had gone astray.

CHORUS

Oh tidings of comfort and joy,
Comfort and joy,
Oh tidings of comfort and joy.

4 Biorhythms

🎧 **10** Do you sometimes feel very happy, while at other times your whole life is under a cloud? Are there times in your life when everything goes wrong? Are there other times when you could climb a mountain with one hand tied behind your back? Some people believe that there are cycles in our lives. At certain times we will feel good. At other times we will feel bad. These cycles are called *biorhythms*.

There are *three* biorhythm cycles: *the physical cycle*, which has 23 days, *the emotional cycle* which has 28 days and *the intellectual cycle* which has 33 days. These cycles start on the day you are born. Each cycle has a *positive* phase and a *negative* phase.

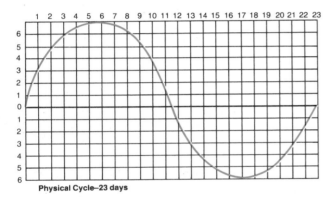

Physical Cycle—23 days

In the positive phase you will feel very healthy and fit.

In the negative phase you will feel lazy. You will get tired easily and you are more likely to become ill.

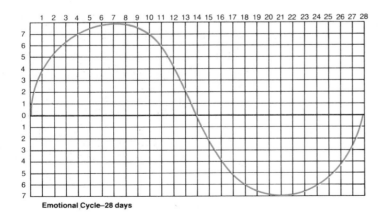

Emotional Cycle—28 days

In the positive phase you will feel cheerful, friendly and optimistic. This is a good time for romance.

In the negative phase you will feel irritable and moody. You will get depressed easily and you are more likely to lose your temper or to cry.

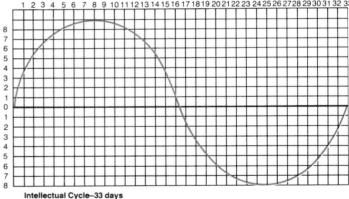

Intellectual Cycle—33 days

In the positive phase you will feel confident. You can think clearly and you can learn things quickly. This is a good time for exams and tests.

In the negative phase you will feel confused. You will not be able to concentrate easily and you are more likely to make mistakes. This is definitely NOT a good time for tests.

The most dangerous times are when the cycle moves from one phase to the other. These are known as *critical days.* Some research in Switzerland showed that 60% of accidents happen on critical days. Some airlines use biorhythm charts. Pilots are not allowed to fly on critical days.

Exercises

1 Read this summary. Most of it is wrong. Correct it.

Biorhythms are rhythms which control our lives. There are five cycles: intellectual, physical, emotional, positive and negative. Each cycle lasts 28 days and each one has a positive and a negative phase. When you are in a positive physical phase you will feel lazy and tired, but you are less likely to become ill. When you are in a negative physical phase you will feel full of energy. The positive emotional phase is a good time for romance. You will feel happy and cheerful. In the negative emotional phase you will not be able to think very clearly. The intellectual phase is very important for school. In the positive phase you will be able to learn things easily but you will forget them very quickly. The negative intellectual phase is the worst time for exams. The best days in the cycles are the critical days. These are the days when the cycle is moving from negative to positive. Accidents are very rare on critical days.

2 Look at the chart:

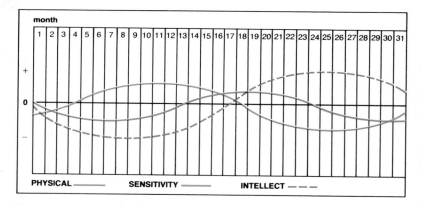

a Which are the critical days on the chart?

b How will the person feel on these dates: 7th, 18th, 25th, 29th?

c Which would be the best or the worst days to:
– get married?
– run a marathon?
– take an English exam?
– have an important business meeting?
– have an interview for a job?
– go for a medical test?
– have a party?

3

Language spot 1

adverbs

a Find all the **adverbs** and **adjectives** in the text.

b Do you use **adjectives** or **adverbs** with the verbs below?

| feel | be | become |
| think | learn | get tired |

c Choose the correct word from the brackets to complete the sentences.

1 I feel (tired/tiredly) today.
2 I can't think very (clear/clearly) today.
3 Do you get depressed (easy/easily)?
4 He has become very (irritable/irritably).
5 You were very (cheerful/cheerfully) yesterday.
6 Old people forget things (easy/easily).

4

Language spot 2

likely to

Say what you are **likely to do**. Match cues from **A** and **B**.

Example

When you are in love, you are likely to feel happy.

A	B
are in love	make mistakes
take exercise	feel healthy
are away from home	get sunburnt
are in a negative phase	die of lung cancer
lie in the sun	feel happy
eat a lot	be fit
smoke	get fat
sleep well	feel homesick
are on a critical day	feel depressed
the weather is bad	things go wrong

5 Your biorhythms

🎧 11 How do you calculate biorhythms? To calculate your own biorhythm cycle you need to know how long you have been alive, i.e. how many days have passed from the day you were born to today. (Include both days.)

This is how you calculate *the physical cycle*. (It's best to use a pocket calculator for this.) We will take as an example someone (*John*) who was born on *22nd June 1950*. Let us assume that today is *17th May 1986*. This is what you do:

1 *Multiply your age by 365.*
John is 35: $35 \times 365 = 12775$.

2 *Add 1 for each leap year.*
Use this chart:

1904	1952
1908	1956
1912	1960
1916	1964
1920	1968
1924	1972
1928	1976
1932	1980
1936	1984
1940	1988
1944	1992
1948	1996

John has lived through 9 leap years:
$12775 + 9 = 12784$

3 *Calculate how many days have passed since your last birthday. Add this to the total.*
From 22nd June 1985 to 17th May 1986 equals 330 days. So 330 days have passed since John's last birthday: $12784 + 330 = 13114$.

4 *Divide the total by 23:*
$13114 \div 23 = 507.1739$

5 *Multiply the decimal remainder by 23.*
(This will give you the day you are at in the cycle.)
$0.1739 \times 23 = 3.999$ (i.e. 4 to the nearest whole number).

6 *Subtract this number from today's date.*

Now you know which day your present physical cycle started. $17 - 4 = 13$ so we know that **John's physical cycle began on 13th May.**

Make a chart like the ones above to show your physical biorhythm cycle.

Example

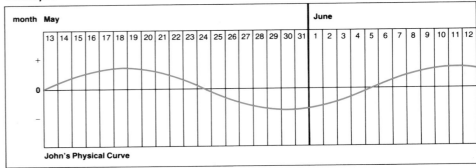

John's Physical Curve

6 Look at John's chart. What will be the *best* and *worst* physical dates for him in the month beginning 13th May.

7

Language spot 3

expressing calculations

a Match the words to the symbols.

multiply	−
subtract	+
decimal point	×
equals	÷
divide	=
add	.

b Listen to the text on biorhythms again. 🎧 11
How do we say these?

$45 + 67$
78×19
$89 - 12$
$78 \div 4$

c 🎧 12 Listen. Write down the problems you hear.
Calculate the answers. Then say them.

Example

$14 \times 56 = 784$

8 How do you think you calculate the other two cycles?

Your life ↓

1 Calculate *the starting dates* of the three cycles for each member of your group.

2 Make a graph of each cycle. Put the cycles of each group member on the graph.

3 Decide which is the best day and which is the worst day for your group to:
– have a class test.
– have sports day.
– receive the results of an exam.

Pronunciation practice

silent letters

a Each of these words has a silent letter. Find the silent letters.

palm tree	scenery
mechanic	guest
bomber	knee
scissors	wrong
knife	autumn
descended	island
ghost	plumber
climb	Christmas
stomach	foreign
half	calm
shipwreck	

b 🎧 13 Listen and check your answers.

c Find more examples of words with silent letters.

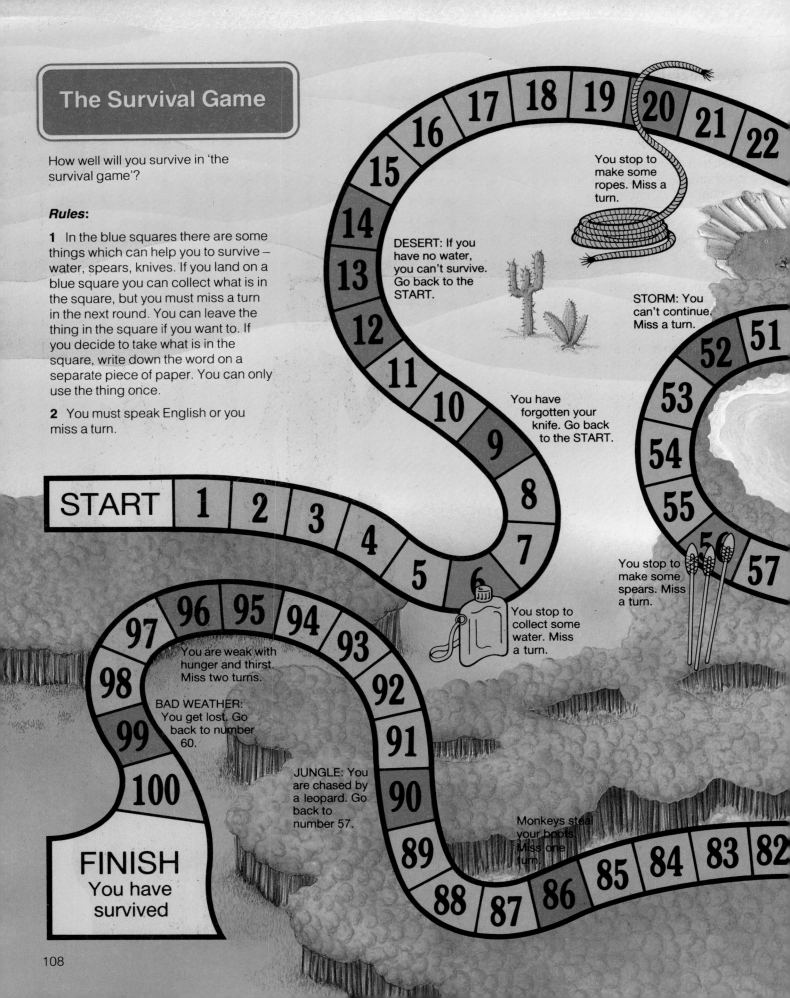

The Survival Game

How well will you survive in 'the survival game'?

Rules:

1 In the blue squares there are some things which can help you to survive – water, spears, knives. If you land on a blue square you can collect what is in the square, but you must miss a turn in the next round. You can leave the thing in the square if you want to. If you decide to take what is in the square, write down the word on a separate piece of paper. You can only use the thing once.

2 You must speak English or you miss a turn.

DESERT: If you have no water, you can't survive. Go back to the START.

You stop to make some ropes. Miss a turn.

STORM: You can't continue. Miss a turn.

You have forgotten your knife. Go back to the START.

You stop to collect some water. Miss a turn.

You stop to make some spears. Miss a turn.

You are weak with hunger and thirst. Miss two turns.

BAD WEATHER: You get lost. Go back to number 60.

JUNGLE: You are chased by a leopard. Go back to number 57.

Monkeys steal your boots. Miss one turn.

START

1 2 3 4 5 6 7 8 9 10 11 12 13 14 15 16 17 18 19 20 21 22

51 52 53 54 55 56 57

82 83 84 85 86 87 88 89 90 91 92 93 94 95 96 97 98 99 100

FINISH
You have survived

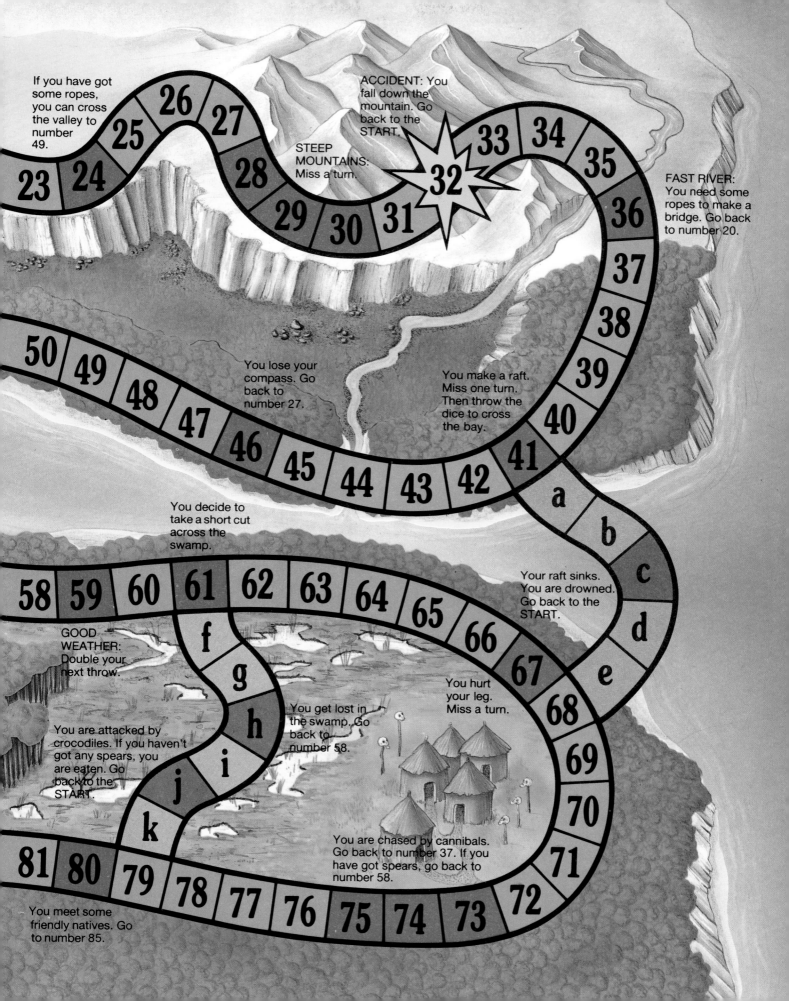

If you have got some ropes, you can cross the valley to number 49.

ACCIDENT: You fall down the mountain. Go back to the START.

STEEP MOUNTAINS: Miss a turn.

FAST RIVER: You need some ropes to make a bridge. Go back to number 20.

You lose your compass. Go back to number 27.

You make a raft. Miss one turn. Then throw the dice to cross the bay.

You decide to take a short cut across the swamp.

Your raft sinks. You are drowned. Go back to the START.

GOOD WEATHER: Double your next throw.

You get lost in the swamp. Go back to number 58.

You hurt your leg. Miss a turn.

You are attacked by crocodiles. If you haven't got any spears, you are eaten. Go back to the START.

You are chased by cannibals. Go back to number 37. If you have got spears, go back to number 58.

You meet some friendly natives. Go to number 85.

Grammar review

PRONOUNS

subject	object	reflexive
I	me	myself
you (sing.)	you	yourself
he	him	himself
she	her	herself
it	it	itself
we	us	ourselves
you (plural)	you	yourselves
they	them	themselves

EXPRESSING A WISH

I'd like I want	to	travel. see the world. have a holiday. be a millionaire.

EXPRESSING INTERESTS

I'm He's She's	not very quite very	good at interested in	sports. practical things. languages. car repairs. art.

PREPOSITIONS WITH FORMS OF TRANSPORT

by in a	plane boat car lorry spaceship submarine ship

by on a	bicycle motorcycle train horse sledge

on	foot

VERBS OF TRANSPORT

ride is used with forms of transport, which you:
- sit on (e.g. horse, bicycle)
- travel in as a passenger (e.g. train, bus, car)

sail is used with water transport (e.g. ship, boat)

fly is used with air transport (e.g. helicopter, plane, spaceship)

sail and **fly** usually mean operating the vehicle, not travelling as a passenger.

drive is used with land transport and ONLY means operating the vehicle.

EXPRESSING AMBITIONS: WOULD LIKE TO

What would you like to do?			
I	would 'd wouldn't	like to	travel round the world. have a big car. be a pop star.

POSSESSIVE PRONOUNS

possessive adjective	possessive pronoun
my	mine
your	yours
his	his
her	hers
its	its
our	ours
their	theirs

QUESTION TAGS

a) The question tag is formed from the auxiliary verb or the verb "to be":

This isn't my book, **is it**?
Jack has got brown hair, **hasn't he**?
That's our train, **isn't it**?
Now we won't be able to go, **will we**?

b) If there is no auxiliary verb, you must use "don't" or "doesn't" for the present tense and "didn't" for the past tense.

You like a challenge, **don't you**?
Kate works here, **doesn't she**?
Carstairs bought the tickets, **didn't he**?

c) When the sentence is **positive**, the question tag is **negative**.

When the sentence is **negative**, the question tag is **positive**.

THE CONDITIONAL TENSE

I You He She We They	would d wouldn't	take the typewriter. leave the pens. get rid of the radio.

What	would wouldn't	I you he she we they	take? get rid of? do? leave?

'IF' CLAUSES 1: FULFILLED CONDITIONS

IF clause	MAIN clause
If we **go** from Dover to Ostende,	it **will take** 3 hours and 45 minutes.
If we **take** the ferry,	it **won't be** very fast.
if you **travel** from Hull,	**will** you **land** in Belgium?

'IF' CLAUSES 2: UNFULFILLED CONDITIONS

IF clause	MAIN clause
If you **were** on a hijacked plane,	**would** you **attack** the hijackers?
If a robber **attacked** me,	**I'd scream**.
If I **had** a million pounds,	**I wouldn't work** anymore.

GERUNDS

a) A gerund is a noun. It is like the present participle of the verb. A gerund can be an object or a subject.

Object:

I like	reading. sleeping. swimming. skating. playing the guitar.

Subject:

Cooking Rock climbing Skiing Fishing Learning English	is easy.

b) Spelling

Verb	Gerund
read	reading
swim	swimming
skate	skating

c) need + gerund

Can you repair this watch, please?
The watch **needs repairing**.

Can you check the brakes, please?
The brakes **need checking**.

GIVING ADVICE

You He She We They	should shouldn't	wait for help. go for help. pray. shout for help. jump out. sit still. pray.

WARNINGS WITH CONDITIONS

If they move, the van | **might** **could** | fall.

If they stay still, another car | **might** **could** | hit them.

PAIR(S) OF

trousers, jeans, knickers, socks: these are always plural. When we want to say how many, we must use **pair(s) of** e.g.

1 pair of socks
5 pairs of tights

ASKING ABOUT AND GIVING SIZES

What size	shoes jumpers shirts	do you take?

I take a size 9.

What is your	collar waist chest	measurement?

It's 81.

RELATIVE CLAUSES

These are the	things places animals	which that	I saw on holiday.

These are the people	that	I met on holiday.

These are the people	who that	helped us.

We use **which** or **that** for places, things and animals.
We use **who** or **that** for people, when they are the **subject** of the relative clause.
We use **that** for people, when they are the **object** of the relative clause.

NON-DEFINING RELATIVE CLAUSES

James V was Mary's father.
James V died when Mary was only one week old.

James V, who was Mary's father, died when Mary was only one week old.

The executioner picked up the hair.
Mary's hair was only a wig.

Mary's hair, which the executioner picked up, was only a wig.

ASKING ABOUT LANGUAGE

What do you call | a place which . . .
something which you . . .
someone who . . .

What is a _ _ _ _ called in English?

EXPRESSING QUANITY

a jar of strawberry jam
4 loaves of bread
2 cartons of yoghurt
1 pound of butter
2 tubs of margarine
2 pounds of rice
3 bottles of milk
1 tin of hot chocolate
4 packets of tea

Uncountable
a little | coffee
a lot of |

Countable
a few | vegetables
a lot of |

COUNTRIES

noun	adjective
America	American
Argentina	Argentinian
Australia	Australian
Austria	Austrian
Belgium	Belgian
Brazil	Brazilian
Canada	Canadian
China	Chinese
Denmark	Danish
England	English
France	French
Germany	German
Greece	Greek
Hungary	Hungarian
Ireland	Irish
Italy	Italian
Mexico	Mexican
the Netherlands	Dutch
Norway	Norwegian
Poland	Polish
Portugal	Portuguese
Russia	Russian
Scotland	Scottish (Scots)
Spain	Spanish
Sweden	Swedish
Switzerland	Swiss

THE PAST PERFECT TENSE

The **past perfect** shows something which happened before the **past**.

Past perfect	Past
Cleo had been a pop singer with a group.	Cleo worked for Canterbury Holidays.
Bruce had lived in Australia.	Bruce lived in England.

EXPRESSING REGRET

I wish I hadn't taken this job.
I wish I had stayed at home.
I wish I hadn't broken the window.

DESCRIBING FEELINGS AND LOOKS

I	feel 'm feeling don't feel 'm not feeling	depressed. worried. well. better. homesick. angry. happy. all right. embarrassed.
He She	looks doesn't look	
You	look don't look	

ASKING ABOUT TV PROGRAMMES

What's on television tonight?
There's a film on BBC2 at nine o'clock.

STATING RULES

Dropping litter Selling drugs Gambling	is	forbidden. prohibited. illegal.

You are not allowed It is illegal	to	drop litter. sell drugs. gamble.
You must not		

These mean the same. "Must not" is informal; the others are formal.

INDIRECT SPEECH 1: STATEMENTS

Tenses

When the reporting verb is in the present tense, the tenses in the reported clause do not change, e.g.

Direct   I work in a shop.
Indirect: She says she works in a shop.
Direct   I'll see Mary, when I go to London.
Indirect   He says he'll see Mary, when he goes to London.

When the reporting verb is in the past tense, the tenses in the reported clause change one tense backwards as follows:

direct speech	indirect speech
present simple	past simple
present continuous	past continuous
present perfect	past perfect
future	conditional
past	past perfect
conditional	conditional
past perfect	past perfect

e.g.

Direct   I work in a shop.
Indirect: She said she worked in a shop.
Direct   I'll see Mary, when I go to London.
Indirect   He said he would see Mary, when he went to London.

Pronouns

Pronouns in the reported clause generally change to the third person, e.g.

Direct   I saw him when I was in England.
Indirect   She said she had seen him when she had been in England.

INDIRECT SPEECH 2: QUESTIONS

Wh– questions

The reported clause has statement word order and begins with the question word:

Where did you buy this camera?

I asked him where he had bought the camera.

Yes – No questions

The reported clause has statement word order and begins with **whether**:

Have you got anything to declare?

I asked him whether he had got anything to declare.

INDIRECT SPEECH 3: COMMANDS AND REQUESTS

Direct   Open your bag, please.
            Come to my office.

Indirect   I asked him to open his bag.
              I told him to come to my office.

EXPRESSING POSSIBILITY

If I had a lot of money, I	would . . . wouldn't . . . would be able to . . . wouldn't be able to . . . would have to . . . wouldn't have to . . .

EXPRESSING POSSIBLE DANGERS

You	might could	get	scratched bitten sunburnt cut burnt stung	by . . .

You	might could	cut scratch sting burn	yourself on . . .

WEATHER FORECASTS

It	's going to will	be	sunny. windy. cloudy. foggy. fine. cold. warm. wet. dry.

It	's going to will	snow. rain.

There	's going to will	be	a thunderstorm.	
			some	rain. snow. fog.

DESCRIBING A PROCESS: THE PASSIVE

Sulphur dioxide and nitrogen oxide **are emitted** by factories, power stations and cars.

Buildings **are damaged** by acid rain.

Pollution **is blown** from one country to another.

CLASSIFYING

An ostrich An oak A lizard	is a kind of	bird. tree. reptile.

SUGGESTING ADVICE

I think we	'd better should ought to	stay here. leave. make a fire.

EXPRESSING REGRET

I We You	should have shouldn't have	stayed near the ship. looked for food. left the ship.

COMPASS POINTS

noun	*adjective*
north	northern
south	southern
east	eastern
west	western
north-west	north-western
south-west	south-western
north-east	north-eastern
south-east	south-eastern

DESCRIBING SHAPES

It's	shaped like a foot. foot-shaped.

It's	shaped like a letter T. T-shaped.

LARGE NUMBERS:

3,657,894: three million, six hundred and fifty-seven thousand, eight hundred and ninety-four.

406,873,241: four hundred and six million, eight hundred and seventy-three thousand, two hundred and forty-one.

PERCENTAGES

Forty-five per cent (45%) of Canada's population have British or Irish ancestors.

Ten per cent (10%) of the people in our class play the guitar.

GIVING ADVICE:

You	should ought to	keep the wound clean. put a plaster on the cut.
Make sure you		keep your arm in a sling. have an X-ray.

EXPRESSING FREQUENCY

once
twice
three times
four times,
   etc.

once a day = every twenty-four hours
twice a month = every fifteen days
three times a year = every four months

USED TO

I You He She It We They	used to	live here. smoke. have a lot of money. drive a fast car. eat too much.

I used to live here. = I lived here in the past, but I don't live here now.

CAUSATIVE 'HAVE': HAVE SOMETHING DONE

Bruce repaired the car. = He repaired it himself.
Bruce had the car repaired. = Someone else repaired the car for Bruce.

ADVERBS OF FREQUENCY

never seldom sometimes often frequently always

Position

a) before the verb:
The farmworker **always** rides a motorbike to work.
b) after "to be"
I am **often** late for school.
c) between the auxiliary and the main verb:
The businessman has **never** ridden a motorbike to work.

RELATIVE CLAUSES WITH 'WHERE'

Stonehenge was a temple.
People worshipped the Sun at Stonehenge.
Stonehenge was a temple where people worshipped the Sun.

DIMENSIONS

A tree 10 metres high

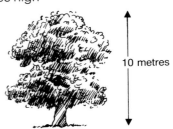

10 metres

A box 4 centimetres long and 2 centimetres wide and 3 centimetres deep

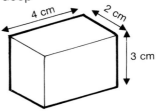

4 cm   2 cm   3 cm

A circle 2 centimetres in diameter

2 cm

A man 1.7 metres tall

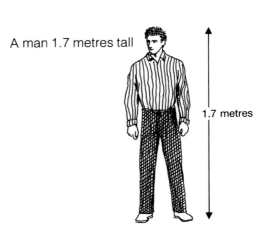

1.7 metres

TIME PREPOSITIONS

in, on, at

in	the fifteenth century 1969 the morning the afternoon the evening February

on	Easter Monday Christmas Day September 9 Friday Thursday July 11 May 18 1876

at	3 o'clock night Easter

PRESENT CONTINUOUS WITH FUTURE MEANING

I'm going to London tomorrow.
The van is coming at seven o'clock.
We're going to the football match on Saturday.
He's leaving next week.

Present continuous + future time expression = definite future

ADVERBS

adjective	*adverb*
I'm angry.	He shouted angrily.
I feel hungry.	She ate hungrily.
He became tired.	He played tiredly.
You look sad.	They talked sadly

EXPRESSING CALCULATIONS

3 − 1 = 2: three minus one equals two

8 + 5: eight plus five

4 × 9:

four	times multiplied by	nine

10 ÷ 2.71: ten divided by two point seven one

Wordlist

This list contains the new words introduced in each unit. They are listed in the order in which they appear.

Introduction

Middle Ages
pilgrim
on the way
tale
I've no idea
group
traveller
entertain
tell
work
interest

run
interesting
hard work
extra
advertisement
boring
a break
expect
guarantee
bored
interested
recent

study
college
university
something different
particularly
interested in
earn
yours sincerely
qualifications
car mechanic
driving licence
repair

pleased to meet you
Canadian student

UNIT 1

1 Ambitions

ambition
by sea
survivor
crew
return
tribesmen
repeat
voyage
solo
circumnavigation
sail
non-stop
complete
bomber
the hard way
via
on foot
sledge

a parking ticket
westwards

2 Carstairs and Carruthers

prize
share
millionaire
on land
enter
get rid of
whole
luggage
go and get
run over
don't worry
black eye

hairdryer
sheet
pillow
sleeping bag
washing powder
soap
shampoo
comb
hairbrush
needle and thread
sewing machine
scissors
penknife
tin opener

3 Planning a route

to land
to cross
crossing
hovercraft

pay
tariff
vehicle
rate
single
return
a half
petrol
distance
overnight

4 Are you a survivor?

calm
nervous
crisis
panic
personality
hijack
attack
sit still
scream
spend
as fast as possible
shipwrecked
desert
hut
fresh
grab
weapon

smell
smoke
the fire
brigade
to faint
owner
probably
risk
emotional
clearly
hero
defend

UNIT 2

1 Mountain View Holiday Centre

view
situated
scenery
originally
country
convert
double
lounge
facilities
provide
canoeing
billiards
cricket
take our word
guest
tremendous
value
teenager
weightlifting
javelin
roller skating
boxing

2 Warming-up

warming-up
activity
stretch
muscle
apart
level with
shoulder
raise
above
elbow
heel
toe
to lower
to flex
rotate
ankle
wrist
spine
hip
to bend
forward
neck

back
waist
knee
forehead

3 The accident

brake
brake shoe
replace
bend
go over
edge
cliff
puncture
out of control
feel sick
to hang
height
sound the horn
jump out
to reverse
roof
pray
hit
axle
rope
tie

headlight
windscreen
smashed
bodywork
scratched
dented
radiator
cracked
bumper
number plate
straighten

4 Carstairs and Carruthers

secret
successful
to travel light
a pair of
size
measure
measurement
try on
continental

waterproof
blouse
boots
swimsuit
slip
gloves
sandals
handkerchief
woollen
sunglasses
nightdress
tube
make-up
bar

long-sleeved
short-sleeved
belt
swimming trunks
pyjamas
razor
shaving cream

collar
bust
chest

5 ZERO G

to wonder
room
space
gravity
zero
problem
float
special
anywhere
fix
go to sleep
upside down
keep fit

spanner
screwdriver
tent

UNIT 3

1 People, places and things

heroine
admire
boyfriend
girlfriend
to dream
to bark
pain

moustache
ice-cream

2 Carstairs and Carruthers

phrasebook
candle
electric
battery

electricity
to cause
volt
adaptor
plug
socket
switch
to switch off
to unplug
appliance

flex
to poke
fuse

3 Food

corn flakes
toast
salad
apple pie
supper
biscuits
jar
strawberry jam
marmalade
honey
carton
plain
rice
lettuce
celery
diet

definitely
in moderation
sweets
pork
shellfish
beef
lamb
oily
garlic
nuts
pineapple
cherry
pears
melon
grape
noodle
fat
contain
bake
grill
roast

4 Languages

tribe
Indo-European
ancestor
homeland
across
distantly related
branch
descended
importance
Roman
Celtic
in contrast
widely spoken

Italian
Catalan
Portuguese
Gaelic
Welsh
Irish
Breton
Swedish
Norwegian
Danish
Icelandic
Dutch
Polish
Bulgarian
Serbo-Croat
Czechoslovakian

Albanian
Ireland
Portugal
Poland
Switzerland
Sweden
Austria
Norway

sidewalk
lift
elevator

UNIT 4

1 Jobs

the previous day
argument
manager
to fire
unemployed
job centre

salary
tip
O-level
preferred
clerk
typist
p.a.
required
including
experience
A-level
minimum
carpenter
training
petrol pump attendant
part-time
receptionist
full-time
hairdresser

2 Nina's problem

round the corner
fault
blame
tear
decision
miserable
go out together
get engaged
depressed
good luck
P.S.
homesick

3 What's on?

the box
cartoon
hits
charts
comedy
thriller
starring
show jumping
western
weather forecast
soap opera
episode
serial

closedown
documentary
lifeboat
opera
current affairs
war
channel
series
play
jazz
acid rain
pollution
flower
science fiction
reptile

4 Mary, Queen of Scots

sad
at the age of 17
mother-in-law
return
jealous
explode
body
strangle
murderer
to suspect
prove
rebellion
go mad
prison
welcome
trust
behead
treason
executioner
wig
father-in-law
brother-in-law
sister-in-law

voice

UNIT 5

1 Singapore

Singapore
lawyer
respect
law
health
prohibited
fine
litter
public
forbidden
a sweet wrapper
a cigarette end
long-haired
to serve
drugs
to possess
illegal
penalty
trafficking
heroin
morphine
death
gambling
official
betting

lottery
permitted
private
jaywalking
pedestrian crossing
apply

2 Matt in trouble

wallet
parcel
to post
helpful
customs
guy
customs officer
to smuggle
under arrest
search
police inspector
to investigate
put on trial
smuggler

3 Carstairs and Carruthers

to charge
evidence
prosecution
defence
judge
guilty
innocent
to sentence
gaol
tricked
verdict
have you got anything to declare?
rabies
cheated

4 Troubleshooter

model agency
smart
attractive
registration fee
fashion
foolishly
busy
patient
blacklist
best-paid
introduce
appear on TV
perfect
face

UNIT 6

1 Paradise Island

paradise
wonderful
coral reef
beach
sound
palm tree
to sunbathe
exactly
equipment

emergency
plenty of
insect repellent
anti-malaria
stomach upset
sterilize
diarrhoea
imported
except for
tool
get sunburnt
get bitten
get stung
suddenly
hurricane
lizard

2 The argument

freezing
ice
thunderstorms
frost
fog
hail
fine
reasonable
agreed
equality
pig-headed
smug
I'm fed up
foggy

3 Trees in danger

serious
elm
threaten
wood
deciduous
oak
beech
birch
coniferous
fir
pine
leaves
trunk
shrink
power station
emit
sulphur dioxide
oxide
substance
water vapour
to form
sulphuric acid
sunlight
oxidant
grow
protect
soil
lungs

4 Carstairs and Carruthers

life jackets
tremendous
to row
marooned
out of sight
snore
asleep

to drift

plan of action

signal

saw
hammer
nails
pair of pliers
screw
axe
plane
spade
rake
file
chisel
paintbrush

5 Maps

bay
isthmus
peninsula
volcano
swamp
jungle
headland
deep
steep
followed
due south
flat
round
bald
beyond
more or less
to lead
turn back

UNIT 7

1 Canada

correct
national
capital
head of state
President
currency
franc
producer
nickel
original
inhabitant

square kilometres
immigrant
Eskimo
fight over
nearly
independent
bilingual
majority
province
flow
goods
mineral
copper
uranium
zinc
agriculture
wheat
cattle
emblem
maple

2 First aid

first aid
fracture
sprain
limb
painful
swollen
discoloured
X-ray
support
sling
patient
bleeding
bandage
plaster
wound
tight
anti-tetanus
injection
eye drops
crepe bandage
pain killers
stretcher
dial
ambulance

3 Carstairs and Carruthers

haunted
midnight
to count
heartbroken
ghost
in bad condition
pretend
frighten
owner
mend
believe in
curtain

pipe
wallpaper
torn
plumber
give us a hand
straightaway
tickle
bang

4 Risk

almost
chances
farmworker
businessman
at risk
daily
machinery
tractor
regularly
non-smoker
nuclear
seldom
accidental
occupation
environment
habits
calculate
involve
snakebite
coalminer
housewife
jockey
building worker

UNIT 8

1 Stonehenge

archaeologist
circle
mystery
prehistoric
ancient
cemetery
grave
monument
observatory
astronomer
witch
magician
sacrifice
god
theory
temple
worship
horizon
ruins
diameter
bank
ditch
gap
consist of
horseshoe
outer
inner
joined
continuous
upright
altar

rectangle
square
triangle

crawl
obstacle
muddy

2 Carstairs and Carruthers

cabin
at sea
get off
excited
disappointed
claim
Boxing Day
gentleman
agreement
divide
share

festival
Easter
Christmas Eve
wedding anniversary
Merry Christmas

3 Christmas

as usual
prepare
turkey
present
carol
doll
reindeer
sleigh
chimney

awake
pillow-case
nowadays
stocking
decorations
underneath
tradition

4 Biorhythms

go wrong
physical
intellectual
cycle
positive
negative
lazy
likely to
cheerful
friendly
optimistic
romance
phase
irritable
moody
lose your temper
confident
concentrate
make mistakes
critical
pocket calculator
assume
leap year
total
multiply
subtract
equal
divide
add

The Survival Game

valley
raft
drowned
spear
take a short cut
cannibal
leopard
hunger
thirst